BEYOND THE SHADOWS
The Light Within

BEYOND THE SHADOWS
The Light Within

Dr. Grace Liverpool-Norris

Published by Victorious You Press™

Charlotte NC, USA

Copyright © 2026 Dr. Grace Liverpool Norris All rights reserved.

No part of this book may be reproduced, distributed or transmitted in any form by any means, graphic, electronic, or mechanical, including photocopy, recording, taping, or by any information storage or retrieval system, without permission in writing from the author except in the case of reprints in the context of reviews, quotes, or references.

Scripture quotations, unless otherwise noted, are taken from the *Holy Bible*, ***New King James Version***®. Copyright © 1982 by Thomas Nelson.

Used by permission. All rights reserved worldwide.

While the author has made every effort to ensure that the ideas, statistics, and information presented in this Book are accurate to the best of his/her abilities, any implications direct, derived, or perceived, should only be used at the reader's discretion. The author cannot be held responsible for any personal or commercial damage arising from communication, application, or misinterpretation of the information presented herein.

TITLE: BEYOND THE SHADOWS

First Printed: 2026

Editor: Dr. Lynn Braxton

Cover Designer: Toyin Badrudeen / Dr. Grace Liverpool-Norris

ISBN: 978-1-959719-64-9

ISBN: (eBook) 978-1-959719-63-2

Library of Congress Control Number Requested:
Ref:MSG1955698_yEWwOABA0pkdVtm0EuTl

Printed in the United States of America

For details email joan@victoriousyoupress.com

or visit us at www.victoriousyoupress.com

DEDICATION

To God be the glory for every word written.

For the ones who taught me love,
The ones who remind me to hope,
And the One who gave me life.

To my husband, my children, my grandchildren, and my brothers
Thank you for your endless love and support.

And in loving memory of my parents,
Whose legacy continues through me.

Acknowledgments

First and foremost, I give all glory and honor to God, who has been my constant source of strength, wisdom, and grace. Every word in this book is a reflection of His faithfulness in my life.

To my amazing husband, Minister Victor Norris, thank you for being my rock and my safe place. Your love and unwavering support have carried me through every season. You believed in me when I questioned myself, and that means more than words can express.

To my incredible children, Shannel and Wesley, thank you for your unwavering encouragement and for reminding me why perseverance is so necessary. You have ignited my spirit to persevere, paving the way for a legacy of faith, courage, hope, and love.

To my stepson, Omani, whether you realize it or not, you have taught me the true meaning of unconditional love: to give it freely, even in turbulent times, and to extend grace when others show up in ways we may not expect or that differ from our own.

To my precious grandchildren, Jayce and Jordyn, you bring joy and light to my life in ways I never imagined. Each of you is a beautiful reminder of God's promises and a reason for me to keep growing and pouring into the next generation.

To my three brothers, Corbett, Andrew, and Gary, thank you for your unconditional love, the joy you bring to my life, and your endless support over the years. You have each played a special role in my life, and I am so grateful for the bond we share.

To my spiritual mentors, thank you for your prayers, wisdom, and guidance. You spoke life into me when I was weary and reminded me of God's truth when I needed it most. Your influence has shaped not only this book but my life.

Special thanks to my professional team from @Victorious You Press my writing coach, the editors, and the graphic designers. Your expertise helped bring this vision to life.

In loving memory of my parents, Donald and Paulette Liverpool, whose lives exemplified unwavering resilience and remarkable perseverance.

Finally, I extend my heartfelt gratitude to each of you who has taken the time to read my words. Your willingness to engage with my thoughts and feelings means the world to me. My deepest prayer is that these pages will serve as a source of hope and healing for your spirit, igniting the courage to fully embrace the incredible strength that resides within you, an inner light waiting to shine brightly in the world. Let this be a reminder that you are never alone, and your true essence deserves to illuminate even the darkest moments.

TABLE OF CONTENT

Beyond the Shadows: The Light Within	1
Introduction	3
A Prayer for the Journey	9
Why I'm Sharing These "Words"	11
Reflection Before Moving Forward	14

PART ONE — 15

1. The Moment I Remembered — 17
2. What I Carried and What I Let Go — 21
3. Letting Go — 31
4. Our Queen — 39
5. Insights — 47
6. When the Past Still Speaks — 57

PART TWO — 63

7. The Turning Point That Wasn't — 65
8. Shadows of Comparison — 71
9. Career Sabotage: Hiding in the Shadows — 77
10. Awakening Strength: The Catalyst for Change — 85
11. The Light That Changed Me — 93

PART THREE — 99

12. Walking in Wholeness — 101

13. Grace That Found Me in the Dark	105
14. The Strength of Surrender	111
15. Stepping into the Light God Always Saw in Me	115

PART FOUR — 119

16. Identity & Anointing	123
17. Moving Forward	129

PART FIVE — 133

18. She is no Longer Silent	135
19. The Hidden Sanctuary	139
20. Lesson Learned: Light After the Fall	143
21. Light After the Shadow	145
22. Let Freedom Reign: A New Beginning	153
23. Equipped for the Journey: Walking in Real Success and Lasting Victory	159
24. The Light Within: Free and Whole	167
A Life Redeemed, A Future Secured	173
What's Coming Next	179
Scripture References	181
About the Author	183

Beyond the Shadows: The Light Within

Uncovering the Light I Was Never Meant to Hide.

"She dimmed her light to survive, but now she shines to thrive. Healing has taught me that wholeness begins in the unraveling."

— Dr. Grace Liverpool-Norris

What happens when we allow our experiences to cast a veil over our inner glow, when we either consciously or unconsciously choose to merge into the shadows? Discovering the light that resides within each of us is not a simple task; it's a profound journey.

When that inner light is finally unveiled, it illuminates the surroundings with a breathtaking radiance, reflecting an unwavering strength and remarkable resilience. In this illuminating moment, the potential for awakening and renewal expands endlessly, inviting a transformational journey into a realm filled with boundless opportunities and vibrant possibilities.

The path to healing has shown me that authentic wholeness often emerges from the intricate process of unraveling. It is a journey where layers of pain, heartache, and past experiences are painstakingly peeled away, revealing the vibrant, authentic self that has been waiting to shine. Each delicate strip away reveals not just the scars but the beauty that exists beneath, inviting us to embrace our true essence.

Introduction

Healing doesn't happen by accident. It takes intention. We must pay attention to the parts of ourselves that are coming undone and take the time to rebuild what has been worn down by life. This rebuilding doesn't begin with striving; it starts with being honest. It takes root when we care for ourselves the way God cares for us—with patience, compassion, and love.

I used to think healing meant becoming someone new. But what I've learned is that true healing is about remembering who I've always been in God's eyes. It means facing the parts of my story I used to avoid, the lack, the self-blame, the shame, the silence, and letting God meet me there. It's in that space, not outside of it, that real transformation begins.

Ezekiel 37:1–10 (New Living Translation) describes a valley filled with dry bones, lifeless, scattered, and forgotten. But God didn't tell Ezekiel to avoid it. He brought him right into the middle of it and told him to speak life into what looked completely dead. That hits home for me because I've been in that kind of place. I've known what it feels like to be empty, stuck, disconnected from myself, and unsure if anything could ever change.

But that valley isn't the end of the story. It's where healing begins. God doesn't skip over our brokenness; He meets us there. And He invites us to do the same. To stop avoiding the pain and start speaking truth into it. To speak life over our broken parts. To speak hope where there's been despair. To remind ourselves that we are still here, still valuable, and still capable of being made whole.

We don't heal by pretending everything's fine. We heal by facing what has been lost, naming what has been buried, and letting God help us rebuild. That means challenging the lies we've believed for too long, the ones that said we weren't enough, or that our story was too messy to matter. It means replacing them with truth: that we are already loved, already worthy, already chosen.

This kind of healing takes courage. It's not about becoming someone new; it's about finally coming back to who we are in Christ: whole, valued, and deeply loved.

This isn't just about recovery. It's about resurrection. It's about taking back the pieces of ourselves we thought were lost—our worth, our voice, our purpose—and allowing God to breathe new life into them.

If you're still reading, I want to thank you. Your willingness to walk through these pages with me means a great deal. This journey we're on, toward healing, wholeness, and reclaiming our identity, isn't easy. But it's necessary.

Together, we're doing the honest work of facing our past, naming our pain, and allowing who we truly are to emerge.

There will be moments when it feels like we're walking through dry and desolate places. Times when we feel like we have nothing left to give. But even in those valleys, especially in those valleys, there is a truth that can anchor us: "I am enough." That truth doesn't come from what happened to us, what we've done, or failed to do. It comes from who God says we are.

In Ezekiel's vision, the dry bones didn't stay broken and scattered; they came together, piece by piece, and came back to life when God breathed into them. That same promise is available to us. No matter how fractured or broken we may feel, healing is still possible. We can be made whole again. Not through quick fixes or surface changes, but through real, profound, lasting transformation, when we let God into the places we've tried to hide or overcome.

This is your time to rise and to shine. To uncover the parts of you that were never meant to stay hidden. To stop shrinking, apologizing, or playing small. Because the truth is, you were never meant to live in the shadows.

Jesus said, "You are the light of the world. A city that is set on a hill cannot be hidden," (Matthew 5:14-15). He didn't say you will be the light. He said you are. That means your light has always been there, God-given, not earned, and it was meant to shine.

Your light has a purpose. It's not about being seen for the sake of attention. It's about showing others the way. Your healing, your story, your very presence, God can use it to bring hope to someone else who's still stuck in the dark.

When we hide our light because of fear or shame, we rob the world of what God wants to reveal through us. But when we own our story and walk in the truth of who we are, we become living proof of God's power to restore what once seemed beyond repair.

So let this be your moment. Not to become someone else, but to fully embrace who you already are. Loved. Whole. And ready to shine.

I hope this book helps you, as it helped me, take a closer look at the deeper reasons we sometimes downplay our worth. It's not always easy to admit when we've been dimming our own light, to stay in the background, to stay safe, or to avoid rejection. But together, we'll work to change that. We're not here to just survive; we're here to shine with confidence, purpose, and truth.

We're no longer shrinking to stay small or hiding in the shadows of our past. We're choosing to stand in the light, even if our voices shake. And even when we find ourselves in hard, uncertain places, we won't see those shadows as something to fear, but as reminders that we're still under the covering of God's protection.

You were created to stand tall, to offer light to others, and to take your place, fully and unapologetically. Your light was meant to do more than flicker. It was intended to guide others, give hope, and leave a lasting legacy.

As with any meaningful journey, I had to build a strong foundation. For me, that foundation was prayer. Talking to God, honestly and consistently, became the anchor I leaned on when I felt overwhelmed, lost, or discouraged. Prayer wasn't just something I did; it became the place where I found direction, strength, and peace. It grounded me through the process of writing this book and reminded me daily of why this journey mattered.

There were times I felt empty, worn out, and unsure of how to keep going. But in those quiet, personal moments with God, I asked him to breathe life back into me. And He did. That's when everything started to shift. I could feel purpose stirring again. I could see that even my broken places had value. I realized God wasn't finished with me, and He's still working in you, too.

That's the kind of transformation this journey offers: not a perfect life, but a renewed one. One that's rooted in truth, lifted by faith, and built on the foundation of knowing you are already enough, and always have been.

Before I could begin writing a single word of this book, I had to pray. Not just once, but daily. Prayer was where I laid down my fears, my doubts, and the pressure to get it all right.

It was where I found the courage to keep going, especially when I felt unqualified, overwhelmed, or stuck.

The following prayer became my anchor, my lifeline. Now, I'd like to share it with you. Whether you're rebuilding your life or simply trying to find your way through a difficult season, this prayer is for you, too. Let it guide you back to the One who knows exactly where you are and how to carry you forward. You don't need fancy words. Just a willing heart. So, take a breath. Let this be your moment to pause and pray.

A Prayer for the Journey

Heavenly Father,

Thank you for giving me the gift of a new day, and with it, the chance to begin again. Thank you for the breath in my lungs, for the dreams stirring in my heart, and for the quiet reminder that it's never too late to step into purpose.

Lord, I come to you with hopes that feel both exciting and overwhelming. There's a fire in me to bring this vision to life, but also fear and uncertainty that sometimes make me question whether I'm capable. Help me not to run from the process. Walk with me through the messy middle, when I'm tempted to give up or talk myself out of what you've called me to do.

Give me the strength to keep going when I feel tired. Give me the focus to stay committed when distractions pull at me. Give me clarity when the words or next steps don't come easily. Breathe new life into the places in me that feel broken or weary. Remind me that I don't have to do this alone, you're right here with me.

Surround me with people who will encourage me, challenge me, and speak life over this dream. Teach me to trust your timing, not to rush ahead or shrink back, but to move forward in faith, one step at a time, day by day, until this vision transforms into reality. Let this work, whatever it becomes, reflect your grace and goodness. Use it to bring light, hope, and healing to others. And through it all, help me to remember I am not doing this for approval, but from a place of already being loved, chosen, and enough.

Thank you for accompanying me on this sacred journey. Thank you for "never leaving me, nor forsaking me." I sometimes struggle to see myself. Thank you for seeing something in me. I surrender this dream, this journey, to you. Lead me as only you can.

In Jesus' name, Amen.

Why I'm Sharing These "Words"

I hesitated to write this part of my story. These words used to haunt me. They were the background noise in my mind for years, words that fed self-doubt, stalled my progress, and convinced me that healing and success were for others, not for me.

But I've come to understand something important: the only way to move forward is to be honest about what has been holding me back. These words, though painful, marked the beginning of my unraveling, and, eventually, my healing. They had been buried deep within me, deep within my soul. Yet, naming the pain gave me power over them.

So I'm sharing them with you, not as a final statement, but as a turning point. Maybe you'll see your struggle in mine, and perhaps it will give you the courage to start naming the lies you've believed, too.

Locked Doors

For years, I was afraid of locked doors, not just physically, but emotionally and spiritually. They represented rejection, closed-off opportunities, and a feeling of being stuck. I never understood why the fear ran so deep, but it shaped how I approached life. I avoided risks. I expected disappointment. I braced for no.

Unworthy

The word that lived closest to me was *unworthy*. It clung to everything I did. No matter how much I achieved or how hard I tried, there was always a quiet voice saying, *You're not good enough. You never will be.* That voice drowned out the truth for a long time.

Shadow

I stayed in the background because it felt safer. I silenced myself to keep the peace. I learned how to disappear without ever leaving the room. Hiding became a way of life, but it came at a cost: I lost touch with who I was.

Shame

Shame was heavy, and it followed me everywhere. It convinced me that my mistakes defined me, that if people really knew me, they'd walk away. But eventually, I got tired of carrying what was never mine to hold. I got tired of believing lies. So I decided to let go.

That's when healing started. Slowly, I began to speak truth over the lies. I allowed myself to be seen and heard. I found my voice. I stopped waiting to feel "ready" and took the first shaky steps toward freedom. This was the beginning of breaking the cycle, of stepping out of self-sabotage and into self-acceptance.

These words might seem simple. But for me, they were powerful enough to keep me stuck for years. They contributed to a pattern of hesitation, fear, and a deep "failure to launch." I believed I was too broken to move forward. But I wasn't. And neither are you.

A Note to You

No matter where your journey starts, healing takes courage. Some days, it will feel impossible. But even when you feel empty, I want you to remember this: **we have prayers.** We have a God who listens, and most importantly, we have a God who answers prayers. And we have each other.

Whether it's my story or yours, what we've lived through matters. Our stories are not just painful memories; they are proof that we survived. And when we speak to them out loud, they become lifelines for someone else.

This is my story. And I share it so you'll feel safe enough to start speaking your own.

Reflection Before Moving Forward

What words, spoken by others or whispered in your mind, have shaped the way you see yourself?

- Take a moment to name them honestly.
- Which ones have held you back?
- Are you ready to let them go?

PART ONE

Chapter One

THE MOMENT I REMEMBERED

I was sitting quietly, staring out the window. Everything felt calm, almost peaceful. But then, out of nowhere, I saw it, like a flash of lightning across my mind. A memory I hadn't allowed myself to remember came rushing back with force. It wasn't new, but it had been hidden, buried somewhere deep. And in that moment, it was as if God had chosen to pull back the curtain and show me something I was finally strong enough to face.

The memory took me back to a place I hadn't thought about in years, a chicken coop. I was five years old. The smell of hay, dirt, and something sour filled the air. The light was barely visible, just thin streaks slipping through the cracks in the wooden slats. It was dark, dusty, and small.

And then I saw it! The shadow of someone standing too close. One hand on the back of my head, holding me in place. My face barely reached his thigh. The other hand moved over himself—his groin—in a slow, deliberate way. I didn't have the right words back then. I didn't know what to call it. But

I knew something was wrong. I didn't understand it at the time, but I knew something wasn't right. I knew I wanted to get out. I knew I felt frozen.

That memory had been buried so deep that I convinced myself it wasn't real. But it was. And naming it, finally saying what happened, was the first step toward healing. What happened in that chicken coop wasn't my fault. It never was.

For years, that memory was locked away, buried beneath silence and time. I never spoke about it. I barely remembered it existed. But when it resurfaced, it brought with it a wave of understanding. It wasn't just about what happened in that coop; it was about everything I had built on top of that buried confusion and fear—the shame, the feeling of being small and voiceless. Suddenly, it all made sense in a new way.

I'm sharing this because I believe in healing. I think that when we tell the truth, especially the complex, hidden truths, we open the door to freedom. For too long, I lived with thoughts that held me down and kept me under a shadow of darkness. They kept me from becoming the person I was always meant to be. But the moment I faced what I had buried, something shifted. And that's why I'm inviting you on this journey with me.

This isn't just about my past. It's about how the past, yours and mine, can shape how we live, love, lead, and show up in the world. When we look at the shadows with honesty and compassion, we begin to see ourselves in a renewed light and reclaim our voice and our power. We can stop hiding. We can stop carrying shame that doesn't belong to us. We can make room for healing, for change, and for the fullness of life that's waiting on the other side of our pain.

So if you're holding on to things you've never said out loud, know this: you're not alone. And you're not broken beyond repair. This is the starting point, not the end. Let's walk through it together.

Chapter Two

WHAT I CARRIED AND WHAT I LET GO

For a long time, I believed the inappropriate behavior I experienced didn't begin until my pre-teen years. But everything changed the day that long-buried memory came rushing back, the moment the light broke through and took me back to the chicken coop. I was just a child, scared and confused, surrounded by the smell of hay, dirt, and the soft clucking of hens. But the most vivid image was the shadow, the figure that had gotten intimately close to this child.

I had buried that memory so deep; I didn't even know it was still there. It was my mind's way of protecting me. But when it surfaced, it hit hard. Everything I thought I knew about my story shifted. It was painful and overwhelming, but it also brought a sense of clarity. What I had avoided for so long was now right in front of me, and I could finally name it.

That shadow had followed me for years. Not just as a memory, but in the way I thought about myself. It crept into my self-esteem, my confidence, my sense of worth. I doubted myself constantly. I held back from opportunities. I silenced my voice. I carried shame that never belonged to me. And for a long time, I didn't even realize it.

But I reached a point where I knew something had to change. I was tired of carrying guilt for something that was never my fault—tired of criticizing myself. Tired of shrinking to make others comfortable. I had to say it: Enough is enough. I chose to stop hiding. I decided to stop blaming myself. I began to fight for my voice, my healing, and my freedom.

For years, I questioned everything. I replayed that moment in the chicken coop over and over, wondering if it was the root of my self-doubt, my fear, the way I kept shrinking back from life. I asked myself the hard, exhausting questions: Was it my fault? Should I have said something? Did I let it happen? That kind of thinking can consume you. It did for a while. I took on guilt that was never mine to carry.

The truth is our culture has taught us to blame the victim. We've all heard the question, "What was she wearing? Why didn't she say no? Why didn't she stop it?" These kinds of questions don't hold the predator accountable. They shame the person who was harmed and leave them feeling responsible for someone else's actions.

I want to ask you something. Just for a moment, pause. Close your eyes. Picture a child you love, your daughter, your son, your niece or nephew, maybe your grandchild, or your younger self. See them laughing, full of light, running through the grass without a care in the world.

Now, imagine someone watching that child—not with love, but with lust, and with the intent to harm. Harm doesn't come only through an obvious act like sexual penetration, but through calculated violations —being repeatedly stalked; an inappropriate sexual touch, whether with hands, an object, or their mouth; lustful stares; or repeated manipulation acts that slowly break down trust. These, too, are violations. They may be subtle, but they are intentional, and they leave deep, lasting wounds, such as fear.

And when the predator is an adult, especially one who seeks out children and hides behind the title of family, the harm cuts even deeper. The danger isn't only from so-called "stranger danger." It is far more devastating when the threat comes from someone familiar— someone a child is taught to trust.

A child should never have to question whether they're safe. No child should be left wondering what they did to deserve harm. Every child deserves to be protected, believed, and defended, especially when the danger comes not from a stranger but from the very person who should have kept them safe and been their shield of protection.

It is a devastating betrayal when the predator wears a familiar face—cloaked in kindness, affection, or authority—dressed in sheep's clothing. This phrase, drawn from Scripture, refers to someone who appears gentle and trustworthy on the outside but whose true nature is harmful, deceptive, and dangerous.

When that predator carries the title of "family," the damage can cut even deeper. It fractures the foundation of trust, distorts love, and leaves a lasting impression on the child's heart and mind. The confusion it creates is not only emotional but deeply spiritual, because the very person entrusted to protect instead became the source of harm.

It leaves a child wrestling with trust, identity, and even their understanding of love and safety. When the protector becomes the predator, it distorts the sacred and shatters the soul's sense of stability. And yet, by the grace of God, even in this kind of brokenness, healing is still possible. Restoration can still rise from the ruins.

That's why I'm telling this story. Not just to process my own pain, but to create a space where we stop carrying shame that never belonged to us. Where we name what happened and let healing begin. Where we remember that our voices matter, and we reclaim the power we were always meant to have.

It was through a moment of divine clarity that the truth surfaced. God allowed me to recall something I had long buried—a truth that changed everything. For most of my life, I believed the abuse began around the age of eight. But I was wrong. The shadow crept in earlier, in ways my young mind couldn't process. Somewhere along the way, I had blocked it out. And for a long time, that silence protected me.

The earliest memory, the one I can no longer bury, began when I was just five years old. By eight, fear had already made itself at home in my body. I remember how the shadow returned again and again, lurking quietly, watching for the moments when I was alone and unguarded. He knew when to strike, during the stillness, while I was playing, just being a child. He sought opportunities to intimidate, to violate, to steal what was sacred. Always subtle, always silent, he moved in the dark corners of my world, where no one else was watching. And I, just a little girl, was left to carry what my heart was never meant to hold. He turned my joy into fear. My laughter turned to silence. Moments that should have been simple or carefree became heavy and confusing.

Even now, I can picture myself peeking down the hallway, waiting to make sure it was safe to come out. I knew what it felt like to be left alone with him, even for ten minutes. My chest would tighten. My heart would race. I would freeze. His touch never felt right, but I didn't know how to explain it. I just knew I wanted it to stop.

The fear was constant, and the weight of it followed me into adulthood. The shadow's presence didn't just violate my body; it also affected how I saw myself, how I trusted others, and how I moved through the world. It took years for me to realize just how deep the damage went. But that moment of revelation, the one God gave me, was the beginning of my healing. It was the first step in reclaiming what was taken and reminding myself that I was never to blame.

I recall another incident, sitting on the soft, worn carpet, surrounded by a colorful array of toys that stood out in dark contrast to the darkened room. As I played, lost in my imagination, a shadow suddenly emerged, mysterious and alluring; it seemed to beckon me to join in a game.

But instead of reaching for the vibrant toys scattered around me, this shadow moved with an intriguing curiosity toward the soft, pink eraser of a pencil resting nearby. With a playful sense of mischief, he began to glide the eraser up and down between my legs, its unexpected movement sparking a mix of emotions and apprehension in my young mind. The shadow's face, disguised as a smile, turned into lust with a smirk. Then, with his other hand, he pressed a finger to his lips, signaling me to remain silent.

I remained silent even in those moments, and on several other occasions as well. In hindsight, I realize the shadow knew precisely what he was doing. Time and again, he committed unspeakable acts against my innocence. However, like a true predator—one who understands his actions but doesn't want to be caught—he always refrained from crossing the line into penetration. Yet, the distinction was irrelevant; the damage inflicted upon my fragile psyche was already profound.

That's the insidious nature of a predator. Just as a skilled hunter stalks its prey with a calculated patience—creeping closer without urgency, navigating the darkness surrounding me, each act leaving a mark on my spirit in ways I could not yet comprehend.

The shadow was more than a memory; it was a looming presence that followed me through the years, twisting my reality and leaving both visible and invisible scars in its wake. It altered how I saw myself, how I trusted others, and how I engaged with the world. Though the choices were never mine, I carried the weight of them as if they were. The silence I kept, whether out of fear, confusion, or the need to survive, became a prison. It locked me inside with the very pain I longed to escape, convincing me that hiding was safer than being seen.

I internalized the wrong that was done to me. I turned it inward, rehearsing the same haunting questions over and over: Did I cause this? Was it something I did? Should I have spoken up sooner? Could I have stopped it? That kind of thinking eroded the truth, wearing me down and distorting my sense of worth.

It wasn't just emotional; it was spiritual. The darkness I carried seeped into my adult life, manifesting as fear, hopelessness, depression, and thoughts I never imagined I'd entertain, such as death. I didn't understand then that I was still trying to survive something my soul had never fully processed.

The pain had settled into the deepest parts of me, shaping how I saw myself, how I trusted, how I loved. I was moving through life, outwardly functioning, but inwardly fractured, still responding to old wounds with silent grief and guarded hope. What happened in childhood had not simply passed with time; it lingered, echoing through my decisions and my relationships. I was still trying to make sense of something that was never meant to make sense, still carrying a weight that was never mine to carry.

I didn't understand yet that I was still trying to survive a battle I never asked to fight.

The burden of "if only" is heavy. It turns pain into self-blame and shame into something we think we deserve. I let those words, if only, follow me for years. They became a weapon I used against myself, chipping away at my confidence and clouding my sense of worth.

The shadow wasn't just someone from my past; it became something I carried with me every day. It lived in my guilt and shame, in the harsh truth that I couldn't forgive myself. It showed up in the choices I doubted, the chances I missed, and the fear that kept me playing small. It became a voice inside me saying, You're too stained to heal. You're too broken to be whole.

That lie settled in deep, convincing me that my pain defined me. I didn't always understand why my thoughts felt so heavy or why joy seemed unattainable. Looking back, I see how shame kept me stuck, how it silenced the truth and fed the darkness. For a long time, I believed my pain was who I was. But I've come to understand that pain is an experience, not an identity. It's not the whole story; it's just one part of the path I had to walk through.

Reflection Questions:

- When have you noticed a voice of shame or self-doubt holding you back from fully stepping into your worth?

- What might change if you began to separate your pain from your identity and embraced the truth that you are more than your past?

Chapter Three

LETTING GO

Healing doesn't always start with a loud breakthrough. Sometimes, it begins with a quiet moment when truth finally rises to the surface, truth we've buried, denied, or weren't ready to face.

Up until then, I had done everything I could to keep moving forward, pushing through life with wounds I couldn't name and emotions I couldn't explain. I had confused silence with strength, thinking that if I didn't speak about what hurt, maybe it would hurt less. But silence has a way of growing heavy. And eventually, it demands to be heard.

When Silence Speaks: The Unseen Weight of What's Left Unsaid

As I look back on those early years, I used to believe that the beatings my grandmother gave the shadow were what turned him into the figure hiding in the chicken coop. But years later, while sitting quietly with no distractions, something shifted. In that still moment, from that memory, I felt what I can only describe as a divine awakening. There was a sudden awareness that hit me hard, clear, and undeniable: the abuse began when I was only five years old.

Until then, I'd carried around a quiet discomfort, a knowing without language. Something had gone wrong in my childhood, but I couldn't quite name it. That day, it became painfully clear. The shadow I had feared as a child wasn't just part of an old story; it was real. And it had stolen my sense of safety before I even had the words to describe fear.

That moment of clarity felt like God revealing the truth to me. It wasn't the first time I had felt God speak to me in stillness, but this time was different. It shook something loose. It permitted me to name the fear, the shame, and the self-doubt I had carried for so long.

Even harder was admitting how much of that shadow I had dragged into adulthood. I had learned to hide, to doubt myself, to shrink. I had learned to self-sabotage before others had the chance to hurt me. That shadow became a means of survival, but eventually, it turned into a way of destroying myself. And now that I can name it, I'm finally beginning to break free.

As I began to peel back the layers of my past, I realized something that changed everything: silence does not mean blame. My silence wasn't consent; it was protection. It was how I survived. For years, I believed that not speaking up somehow made it my fault. I wish I had known earlier that my pain didn't reflect who I was; it reflected what was done to me. Maybe then, I could've saved myself from the self-destruction, the wasted years, and the opportunities for healing I didn't think I deserved.

Let the Unraveling Begin.

As I began to peel back the layers of my past, I finally realized something that changed everything: silence does not mean blame. My silence wasn't a choice I made freely; it was how I survived. For years, I carried the weight of what had happened to me, believing that not speaking up somehow made me responsible. I wish I had understood sooner that my pain didn't reflect my worth; it reflected the damage caused by years of predatory actions. If I had known that I wasn't to blame, maybe I could have saved myself from the self-destruction, the wasted years, and the missed chances to begin healing.

Letting go of the guilt was one of the most powerful things I have ever done. It was the beginning of reclaiming my life. I had to dig deep to unlearn the lies that had shaped how I saw myself. I made a decision: I would no longer live as a product of someone else's darkness. I would not let their actions define me. Instead, I chose to believe in the truth of who I was becoming, a resilient, victorious woman who refused to stay hidden in the shadows of shame.

The real failure wasn't found in my silence. It was believing the lie that I was meant to carry the burdens that never belonged to me. Yet even that misunderstanding became part of my healing—because once I recognized the truth, I realized that God never intended for me to carry what He came to lift.

With that clarity came a deeper understanding of how those early traumas shaped every part of me, how I saw myself, how I related to others, and even how others, especially men, perceived and treated me. However, the most powerful shift came when I began to see myself through God's eyes. Where I once saw shame, He showed me grace. Where I felt unworthy, He spoke love.

This is where the real healing began, with self-love, self-forgiveness, and trusting that God's promise is true: I am more than enough. I find comfort in the words of Scripture: "And He said to me, 'My grace is sufficient for you, for My strength is made perfect in weakness.' Therefore, most gladly I will rather boast in my infirmities, that the power of Christ may rest upon me," (2 Corinthians 12:9).

Reflection: When Silence Speaks

Before you move on, take a moment to sit with what has been uncovered. Sometimes, the loudest parts of our story are the ones we've never spoken out loud. Silence, while once a survival tool, can quietly shape how we see ourselves, how we love, and what we believe we deserve.

Reflection Questions:

- What unspoken experiences or emotions have shaped your story?
- In what ways has silence protected you? In what ways has it held you back?
- Are there beliefs or burdens you've been carrying that were never truly yours to hold?
- What truth is God gently inviting you to face, not to harm you, but to heal you?

Take a moment to write down what rises inside of you. There is no pressure to have it all figured out. This is your space to begin loosening the grip of what's been left unsaid.

Chapter Four

OUR QUEEN

Real healing began when I stopped running from the damage caused by the shadow and finally faced the deeper wounds underneath my feelings of unworthiness. I started to uncover the root of my pain, learned to give myself love, and chose to forgive, not just others, but myself. And little by little, I began to believe that God's promises weren't just for everyone else; they were for me, too. I am enough, even with the cracks.

That truth settled into my spirit and gave me strength I didn't know I had. But before I could fully see myself through God's eyes, I had to look back, with honesty and compassion, at the first woman who shaped my view of love, strength, and survival—my mother.

As we move deeper into my story, it's important to understand the family and cultural backdrop that shaped much of my early life. The silence around bodies, boundaries, and difficult topics didn't happen by accident; it was woven into the fabric of my upbringing. To truly grasp how the past influenced my sense of self, I need to share what it was like growing up in my family, the values passed down, and the unspoken rules that often kept pain hidden. This chapter opens a window into that world, a world where love and discipline often came wrapped in silence, and where trauma quietly shaped the generations before me.

Before I ever understood what sacrifice meant, I saw it lived out in my mother. Her strength wasn't loud, but it was constant. She carried burdens she rarely spoke of and dreams she often set aside, just so we could move forward. She wasn't perfect, and neither was her love, but she showed up in the ways she knew how. This chapter is a reflection on her life, the choices she made, and how they shaped ours.

Our mother, our queen, was the heart of our family. She was the one who dared to step into the unknown so her children could have a shot at something more. Our parents didn't go to church during those years, not because they didn't believe, but because survival took priority. They were working, striving, doing what they could with what they had.

It was our mother who made the bold move first, leaving the only home we knew in Guyana to begin a new life in the United States. She left behind everything familiar so she could build a foundation for our future. While she was gone, my siblings and I stayed behind with our father and grandmother. Our father worked long, exhausting hours, leaving our day-to-day care mostly in our grandmother's hands.

Looking back, I see now how deeply those years affected her, how the loneliness, separation, and constant pressure shaped the woman she became. Her love was always there, but it didn't always look the way we expected. It was strong, steady, but often silent.

During that time, our grandmother became our primary caretaker. She was firm, no-nonsense, and deeply traditional. We were raised with the unspoken rule that children should be seen, not heard. There were no bedtime stories or long embraces, only structure, discipline, and survival. I often found myself longing for softness, for comfort, for a mother's warmth. But even then, I knew my mother's absence was not abandonment. It was love, expressed through sacrifice.

I want to pause and hold space for something sacred. There was a pivotal moment with my mother, one I'll share more fully later, that revealed the quiet, powerful way she expressed love. Though she didn't always show affection in ways I could easily recognize as a child, I would come to see that she wasn't lacking in emotional support. Her love was steady, even if silent. That moment helped me understand her better and helped me see how her way of loving shaped the way I respond to my daughter. Her silence, her strength, and her sacrifices became a part of how I had mothered, but also a part of what I've had to unlearn.

Despite the deep love and appreciation my siblings and I shared for our queen, our beloved mother, I've come to realize how her life, and ultimately her death, left an imprint far deeper than I understood at the time. She was the center of our world, the quiet force that held us all together. Her warmth was constant, her love fierce. She gave all she had without asking for anything in return, often silencing her own needs to care for everyone around her.

Growing up, I don't recall her ever voicing a complaint. As a child, I saw a woman who smiled through everything. But as an adult, I see more clearly. I see the layers she carried, worries she never spoke, pain she never shared. She endured much more than we knew. Her strength was not loud or obvious; it was a silent resilience, the kind that goes unnoticed until it's gone.

Her early passing, at just forty-eight years old, shattered everything my brothers and I thought was stable. Breast cancer took her from us, but at the time, we didn't fully understand what was happening. We had no language for grief, no preparation for the loss. During her illness, we remained mostly unaware of the depth of her suffering. She kept smiling, kept showing up, shielding us from the worst of it, even as her body failed her. That decision, though protective, left me wrestling with her absence long after she was gone. I didn't know how to grieve a pain I had never been allowed to see, at least until it was too late.

On March 10th, in the stillness of the early morning, everything changed. I was just weeks away from turning twenty when my brothers and I witnessed something we will never forget. Around 3 a.m., barely being able to move for the past few days, our mother suddenly got out of bed with surprising strength. It felt otherworldly, like something sacred had stirred. We rushed to her side and found her slumped forward, her body giving way. We lifted her back to bed, where she took her final breath.

Looking back now, through the eyes of faith, I no longer believe that moment was random. I believe God gave her that last surge of strength for a reason, a divine release. One final act of will, a final act of grace, of dignity, a glimpse of the strength that had carried her through so much, before her divine release. God gave her just enough strength to rise one last time before calling her home.

Losing her changed me, as I know it changed the perspective of my brothers' lives as well. I carried grief I didn't know how to name. I wore her strength like armor, but also inherited her silence. For years, I tried to be strong like her, but I didn't yet understand that strength isn't just about endurance. It's also about healing, softness, and allowing yourself to be seen.

Her legacy lives on in me, not just through her sacrifices but through the silence she carried. The love she gave was real, but it was often unspoken, shaped by the affection she never received from her mother. That quiet strength became the way she loved us, but it also left unanswered questions, a sense of distance, and a longing I couldn't name for years. Her emotional restraint became part of my own story. I, too, learned to be silent, to endure, to push through without always understanding why. As I began to unpack that silence, I realized that honoring her doesn't mean repeating her patterns; it means breaking them with love. In honoring her, I also gave myself permission to be seen, to feel, and to heal.

Reflection: Inheriting Silence, Choosing Healing

Sometimes, the strongest people in our lives loved us the best way they knew how, even if it was quietly, guarded, or without affection. That silence, while meant to protect, often becomes a pattern we carry into adulthood.

Reflection Questions:

- In what ways did your mother or caregiver show love? Were those expressions nurturing, or silent, strong, and self-sacrificing?

- How have those early experiences shaped how you express (or withhold) your own emotions?

- Are there unspoken patterns, like silence, emotional distance, or over-responsibility, that you've inherited?

- What would it look like for you to honor your mother's sacrifices while also giving yourself permission to feel, speak, and heal?

Write freely. There are no wrong answers here. This is your space to begin making sense of the silence—and breaking the patterns that no longer serve you.

Chapter Five

INSIGHTS

Healing often asks us to revisit places we've tried to forget. After learning to understand my mother's silence and breaking the patterns I inherited from her, I had to face a deeper layer—the places where silence wasn't a choice but a force. The places where fear lived, where innocence was stolen, and where a child was left to make sense of things far too dark for her age. That's where the absolute unraveling began.

Insight from the Past

The routine rarely changed. Whenever my parents stepped out, I would wait, sometimes nervously, for the words, "We'll be back." Too often, I was left behind while they went to run errands or support my brothers at their games. What they didn't realize was that I was being left with the shadow, someone they trusted, someone who slowly stripped away my sense of safety.

Each time they left, I felt fear rising in my chest. I knew something was wrong, even if I couldn't explain it back then. Sometimes, I locked myself in my room and waited. Other times, I would reach for the house phone, mounted between the kitchen and the living room, and frantically call a friend, hoping the sound of a voice on the other end might protect me. But the phone couldn't follow me into the safety of my room. And the shadow always waited for the moment I let my guard down. I tried to create small shields, locked doors, phone calls, and distractions, but they were never enough to protect me. The shadow grew bolder when no one was watching. And no matter how hard I tried to hide, the fear always found its way in.

I would often pick up the house phone, hoping that the familiar sound of one of my friends' voices would keep the shadow at bay. Yet even that distraction sometimes faltered. Each time I believed the coast was clear to venture out of my room for whatever reason, there it was, the shadow, lurking in the dim light, poised to overtake me like a predator stalking its prey, patiently waiting for the perfect moment to strike.

I distinctly remember a small step stool, more like a mini ladder, we kept in the kitchen to reach the high shelves of our cabinets. One day, I found a flicker of courage and decided to brave the kitchen for a snack. As I stood at the top of the ladder with my hand stretched up to grab a treat, I suddenly felt the lurking presence of the shadow and an insistent whisper in my mind saying, "Please don't."

In that fleeting moment, every ingenious defense strategy I had meticulously crafted to outwit the looming shadow evaporated from my mind, leaving me momentarily paralyzed. My adrenaline surged, drowning out my thoughts, as I faced the figure before me, its very presence creating fear. That was the moment that I lost my voice. I felt powerless against its relentless whispers, designed to keep me enveloped in darkness and vulnerability, as I felt wetness pressing against my womanhood, even though I was only a child.

My young mind struggled to grasp the whirlwind of events unfolding before me. Everything felt surreal, as if I were watching a scene from a distant dream, or maybe it was happening to someone else. Yet, even at that young age, a deep instinct stirred within me, whispering that something was very wrong about this. This wasn't how families engaged with each other. A sense of shame filled me, and I knew, with a clarity that belied my years, that this was not supposed to happen.

As I write this now, with tears tracing paths down my cheeks, I mourn the loss of my innocence, the fragrant blooms of childhood crushed beneath that weight of fear. My heart aches for that frightened girl, embodying all the self-doubt and shame that I grew to know intimately. It's as if those feelings wove themselves into the very fabric of my being.

Imagine, if you will, a little girl trying to evade a shadow for years, hiding and stifling her fears in the corners of her mind. I learned from early on how to suppress myself, turn any attention away from me, and hide in the shadows. Being stalked by a predator within the shadows left this little girl unworthy, insecure, afraid, and vulnerable to other predators. I was convinced that the stain etched upon my skin would be a permanent reminder, a lasting imprint that I would carry with me for a lifetime.

The cycle of evasion needed to end. One day, while sitting in the nurse's office at my middle school, around eighth grade. I met a kind-hearted nurse. She exuded an aura of warmth that drew me in, a gentle presence that enveloped me in a sense of safety. For reasons I couldn't quite pinpoint, I felt comforted enough to share my secret, that something malevolent was happening at home, and that I didn't know how to voice it to my mother. I remember her patient gaze and reassuring demeanor as she listened without demanding details. Instead, she simply encouraged me to trust my mother and to open up to her, planting a seed of hope in my heart that perhaps a beam of light could finally break through the shadows.

Reflection Question: A Seed of Courage

Think back: Who offered you a moment of safety when you needed it most? And how might you continue nurturing the seed of courage that was planted in that moment?

Sometimes, the first step toward healing isn't a full confession—it's a whisper. It's finding the strength to say something to someone who makes you feel safe, even if you can't explain it all.

Journal Prompt:

Think about a moment when you felt seen, heard, or safe, no matter how small it seemed at the time. Who was there? What did they say or do that helped you feel that way?

Now ask yourself:

- What did that moment awaken in you?
- Have you allowed yourself to revisit or build on that courage since then?
- What would it look like to honor that younger version of you by continuing to speak up, even if your voice trembles?

Swept Under the Rug

Breaking the silence takes courage, but what happens when your courage is met with more silence? After years of carrying the weight alone, I finally found the strength to speak. I hoped that once the truth was out, healing would begin. But what followed taught me something even more difficult to face: not everyone knows how to express their pain, even when they love you.

I still remember the moment I decided to tell my mother about the shadow that had stolen my safety. I was young, but I knew what courage felt like, and I knew this was it.

She was standing at the kitchen sink, washing dishes. I stood nearby, heart racing, counting silently in my head. I was terrified, but I held on to the school nurse's gentle words: "Trust your mother." So I took a deep breath and said quietly, "Mom, I have to tell you something."

She stopped and turned toward me. "What is it?" "I'm afraid of the shadow," I said. She looked confused. "What shadow?" "The one that tries to touch my private parts." Her face didn't change much. She turned back to the sink and said, "I'll take care of it." That was all.

No questions. No hug. No space for tears. No "Are you okay?" or "Tell me what happened." Just silence, and then, dishes.

It took me a long time to understand what that moment meant. At the time, I felt dismissed, unsure, and even more alone. But as I got older, I began to see the layers beneath her reaction. My mother came from a world where survival didn't leave much room for emotion. She didn't have the tools to respond differently because her mother hadn't equipped her with them.

Today, we might call it emotional unavailability, but back then, it just felt like love wrapped in practicality. She kept food on the table, made sure we were clean, clothed, and safe in the physical sense. But there were no bedtime talks, no affirming words, no comforting touch. Her love was quiet and task-oriented. It showed up in action, but not in conversation. And when I needed words the most, there were none. One cannot pour from an empty cup.

The following day, I stumbled upon my father locked in a heated argument with a dark figure that hovered in the corner of the room, its features indistinct and shifting like smoke. The figure appeared only as a shadow, but was unrecognizable to me. The tension in the air was palpable, electric with unspoken words. Before I could fully grasp the situation, the shadow seemed to dissolve into thin air, leaving behind an unsettling silence.

No questions were asked, and no explanations were offered to my three brothers or me. We were left to navigate the disarray of emotions and confusion, piecing together the fragmented images of what had just unfolded. The air was thick with an unspoken weight of mystery, a palpable tension that seemed to wrap around us like a heavy fog.

The shadow that had loomed over my life was suddenly banished, yet its lingering effects clung to me, haunting my thoughts. The absence of that foreboding presence was stark, but the echoes of its influence remained with me for far too long, shaping my future in ways I could hardly comprehend.

Reflection: When Love Isn't Loud

Sometimes, the people we hoped would protect us simply didn't know how. They may have loved us the best way they knew, through action, structure, or provision, but their silence or inaction, unintentionally, sometimes cause wounds. Naming that truth doesn't mean dishonoring them; it means being honest about what we needed and didn't receive. That's where healing begins.

Journal Prompt:

- Think of a time when you needed emotional support but didn't receive it.
- How did that moment shape your understanding of love, trust, or safety?
- What did you need to hear or feel in that moment?
- How might you begin offering those things to yourself now, through your words, actions, or boundaries?

Chapter Six

WHEN THE PAST STILL SPEAKS

I had hoped that speaking up would bring closure. That naming the truth would finally silence the pain. But instead, the silence that followed only made the past feel more alive. It lingered in my body, in my decisions, in the way I moved through the world. I realized that even though I'd finally said the words out loud, the real wound wasn't born of what had once been said to me; it was born of what had never been said back. That's when I began to understand: the past doesn't disappear just because we try to forget it. It shows up until we're ready to face it.

Growing up, I often heard people say, "Your past doesn't matter." I wanted that to be true. I held tightly to the idea that if I could just keep moving forward, if I worked hard enough, stayed busy enough, I could outrun the pain, the dysfunction, the memories. For a long time, that became my survival plan. Bury it. Push past it. Don't look back.

But life has a way of bringing things full circle. The past doesn't stay buried. It surfaces in unexpected triggers, in relationships, in the quiet moments we try to ignore. I started noticing how the weight of what I hadn't dealt with showed up in my reactions, my insecurities, and my inability to trust or receive love.

That's when I had to face the truth: my past does matter. Not because it defines me, but because it shaped me. It taught me how to survive, but not how to heal. And if I wanted to stop reliving it, I had to stop pretending it didn't exist.

The way I downplayed myself, how I viewed myself, and how I handled relationships and responsibilities were all connected to my earlier experiences. I wasn't just making choices in the present; I was responding to old wounds, old fears, and patterns I didn't know I was repeating. Ignoring my past didn't free me from it, it just gave it more quiet power over my life.

I started to see a pattern. Every time I got close to something good—success, recognition, even peace—I would pull back. I would shrink, downplay my abilities, and let others take the lead. I convinced myself that it was humility, or that I didn't need the spotlight. But deep down, I was afraid. Afraid to be seen. Afraid to believe I was worthy.

That fear started young. It followed me like a shadow, always there, just behind me. Not loud, but persistent. It fed on my silence and doubt. It wasn't just about the past anymore; it had taken root in how I saw myself.

It wasn't until I stopped running from it, until I faced what had shaped me, that I began to change. Healing didn't mean pretending the past didn't happen. It meant acknowledging it, understanding it, and deciding it wouldn't define me anymore.

Reflection Questions:

- In what ways is your past still speaking into your present?
- What recurring patterns or responses in your life might be rooted in past experiences, and how have they shaped the way you see yourself, your worth, or your potential?

Journal Prompt:

- Take a moment to reflect on your current habits, reactions, or feelings that might trace back to your past.
- Can you identify any recurring patterns that show up in your relationships, work, or self-talk?
- How might these patterns be connected to experiences you've had before?
- What would it mean for you to begin recognizing these influences without judgment, and how could that awareness open the door to new choices?

In summary, Part 1 was about unraveling the roots of my pain, the silence I inherited, the shadows I carried, and the moments I first found the courage to speak. But understanding where I came from was only the beginning. The next chapter of this journey isn't about sudden breakthroughs or instant healing. It's about the slow, messy process of facing what I thought would be a turning point, and discovering that sometimes, real change takes longer than we expect.

PART TWO

Chapter Seven

THE TURNING POINT THAT WASN'T

I remember my high school graduation as if it were yesterday. It should have been a day full of pride and joy, but instead, I felt numb and detached. I told my mom I didn't feel like going. On the surface, it sounded casual, but inside, I was torn.

I did want to be there. My closest friends were excited, and part of me wanted to celebrate with them. But I didn't say that. Instead, I shut down and pretended not to care.

The truth was, I was struggling with deep insecurity and self-doubt. After years of being overshadowed, first by the threats that lurked unseen, then by the critical voice I learned to carry inside, I had started to believe I wasn't worthy of being seen or celebrated. I'd learned to dim myself to stay safe.

What I needed in that moment was reassurance. I wanted my mother to gently push back, to remind me that I mattered, that this moment mattered. But instead, she quietly accepted what I said. I think she sensed something was wrong, but didn't know how to respond.

That was the day I started slipping further into the shadows, not the one that chased me, but the one I created for myself. It was safer there. At least, that's what I believed at the time.

Graduating from high school wasn't just the end of a chapter; it was the start of a deep, personal battle with self-worth. I still remember that day clearly. It was supposed to be a milestone, something to be proud of. My two best friends were excited, ready to walk across that stage, and deep down, I wanted to be there too. But when I told my mom I didn't feel like going, she didn't question it. She simply said, "Okay." No urging. No encouragement. Just a quiet agreement.

That moment stuck with me, not because she meant harm, but because I was already so unsure of my value that her silence felt like confirmation. I needed someone to see past what I said and hear what I couldn't voice. I needed to be told, "You belong there." But instead, I began to believe I didn't.

That day marked the beginning of me shrinking myself. I had earned my diploma, but it felt invisible to me. No celebration. No recognition. I told myself I didn't deserve any of it. The shadow I lived under began with the predatory actions that targeted me as a child, but over time, I took on that shadow myself. I started believing I was unworthy, invisible, and I allowed that darkness to follow me, even when the threat was no longer there. I was no longer just being dimmed by outside forces. I had started doing it to myself.

For years, I let insecurity speak louder than truth. I played small. I kept quiet. I kept striving for affirmation, even though deep down, I didn't believe I was worthy of it. Beneath all that effort was a quiet ache, a longing to be seen, not for my accomplishments, but simply for being me.

It took time to break free from the patterns I had lived in for so long, patterns rooted in fear, striving, and self-doubt. Healing didn't happen overnight. It required deep faith, honest self-reflection, and a willingness to confront the lies I had believed about myself. But the real transformation began when I encountered Jesus, not as an idea, but in a deeply personal way. I didn't just learn about his love, I felt it. And through that relationship, I finally realized I didn't have to crouch in the shadows, shrink myself, or keep performing to prove my worth. I was already enough—not because I earned it, but because He said I was.

When I look back now, I don't see my high school graduation as a failure. I see it as another turning point, a difficult one, yes, but a turning point, nonetheless. I wandered for a while, carrying silence and insecurity longer than I needed to. But I didn't stay stuck there. Bit by bit, I found my way forward.

By letting go of the false version of myself shaped by fear, I began to discover the woman God had always intended me to be. I no longer live in those shadows. I walk fully in the light of who God says I am, a light that doesn't flicker, fade, or shrink.

This is the woman I was always meant to become: whole, valued, and no longer afraid to step out of the shadows.

Reflection:

Sometimes, what feels like failure or missed opportunities is actually the start of a new path. It's okay to take time, to wander, and to struggle. Healing and growth aren't linear; they happen in fits and starts. What matters is that we keep moving toward the light of who we truly are.

Journal Prompt:

- Think about a moment in your life that felt like a setback or failure.
- How might that moment have been a turning point in disguise?
- What parts of yourself did you begin to discover or reclaim after that time?
- How can you remind yourself that growth is a process, not a destination, and that you are becoming the person you are meant to be?

Chapter Eight

SHADOWS OF COMPARISON

Before I could truly heal, I had to face the damage left behind by being preyed upon. For a long time, I believed something about me, especially as a young girl, made me an easy target. I carried this belief silently, convinced it was my vulnerability, my presence, or some invisible mark that made certain men see me as prey.

I still remember walking to my middle school one morning with my two best friends. We were heading down the street when a man known around the neighborhood for his erratic behavior started walking toward us. We instinctively linked arms, forming a line as a kind of shield. "Keep walking," we told each other.

As he got closer, he forced his way through our linked arms. As he passed, he suddenly reached out and grabbed my breast. It unfolded in an instant, too fast for my young mind to comprehend. I tried to brush it off with nervous laughter and uncomfortable silence. But what my friends didn't realize was that I couldn't simply brush it away or forget it.

That single moment burrowed deep inside me and became part of my quiet shame. I asked myself, Why me? Why was I the one he chose? Was I the weak one? Could he sense something broken in me, something still visible from the pain I carried from my past?

Another time, around my high school era, I was riding a train into New York City. A man sat across from me. I noticed his behavior shift, and before long, he began touching himself. I couldn't look away. It was as if I were frozen, stuck in the moment, unable to move or react. It felt like he knew I wouldn't. Like he was testing my silence. Once again, I blamed myself. I believed that my vulnerability invited this, that somehow, I gave off something that made men think they could violate my space.

Those moments stayed with me. Each one layered onto the next, building a narrative in my mind that I was vulnerable, a target, and somehow to blame. The shadow of my past followed me. It shaped how I saw myself, covered in shame, drowning in silence, and struggling to breathe under the weight of unworthiness.

Years later, as a married adult to my now ex-husband, and a mother, I took my children to Brooklyn to visit their grandmother. One of their uncles, my ex-husband's brother, lived in the same brownstone house. While the kids were spending time with their grandmother and cousins, I ended up in another part of the house, talking with my brother-in-law. The conversation turned personal, and as I opened up about the pain of the divorce, I began to cry. He leaned in to hug me, which I assumed was a gesture of comfort. But as I pulled away, he forced his tongue into my mouth.

I didn't tell my ex-husband what happened. I didn't trust how he would respond. He had a volatile nature, and I feared he would blame me instead of holding his brother accountable. Deep down, I believed his brother had seen my vulnerability and exploited it.

This and the other incidents mentioned before were not the only times I experienced this kind of violation. I can remember at least two doctors who made inappropriate advances toward me during routine exams. One pressed his groin against my legs while examining me, refusing to shift his body. I froze. I didn't say anything. I didn't speak up for myself. In that moment, once again, I became voiceless.

And I wish I could say it all stopped there—that these things happened in the past, long ago. But the truth is, they didn't. More recently, I went in for a doctor's appointment, and again, the boundaries were crossed. The physician leaned in too close, pressing his groin against me while using his stethoscope, repeatedly placing it near my breast in a way that felt calculated and inappropriate. His posture, his silence, and the lingering closeness all sent a message. Afterward, he seemed annoyed, almost disappointed, as if expecting a reaction from me that I didn't give. Once again, I said nothing. I stayed silent.

These moments have left a deep mark. They've reinforced the message that my body is vulnerable, that my voice doesn't matter, and that I'm somehow responsible for the way others choose to treat me. They've shaped a distorted image of how men see me, and how I see myself.

The belief that I give off something, some kind of weakness, has followed me for years. It's made me question my worth, my safety, and my ability to be seen as more than someone to be used or dismissed. These feelings of inadequacy and shame have lingered like an unwanted shadow, appearing in quiet moments, crowded rooms, and the deepest parts of my thoughts.

There have been times when it felt like too much—like the weight of it all might swallow me. The pressure to hold it together, to keep going, to not make a scene, or to not remain in a state of depression that I sometimes feel myself slipping. It has been overwhelming. And if I'm being completely honest, there are still days when that old shadow returns—the one that tells me I'm not enough. That I'm not safe. That my voice doesn't carry weight.

Reflection: Facing the Shadows Honestly

Healing doesn't always mean the shadows disappear for good; it means learning how to face them with honesty and compassion when they return. The lies we believed about ourselves, especially those shaped by trauma, can still echo in our minds. But every time we name them, every time we refuse to agree with them, we take back a little more of our power. You are allowed to have hard days. What matters is knowing the shadow doesn't define you anymore.

Journal Prompt:

- Think about the thoughts or beliefs that still arise when you're feeling vulnerable.
- What lies or "old shadows" try to creep in during those moments?
- Where did those beliefs begin, and how have they affected the way you see yourself today?
- What truth do you need to speak over those lies right now? Write it out as if you're talking directly to the younger version of you who first started carrying that weight.

Chapter Eight

CAREER SABOTAGE: HIDING IN THE SHADOWS

Naming the shadows was only the beginning. I had to come face-to-face with how they continued to shape my everyday life, especially in the places where I was supposed to shine. Healing wasn't just about looking back at the pain of the past. It was about recognizing how those wounds had followed me into adulthood, quietly influencing the choices I made, the risks I avoided, and the dreams I silently buried. One of the most painful areas where this showed up was in my career.

For much of my professional life, I let fear and self-doubt guide my decisions. Whenever a leadership opportunity came my way, I backed away, not because I lacked the skill, but because I didn't believe I was worthy of the role, that I wasn't qualified. I convinced myself it was easier and safer to stay in the background.

Opportunities would appear in promotions, invitations to speak, chances to lead, and to have a voice. But I consistently found reasons to step aside. I told myself someone else was better suited, more qualified, or more confident. I told myself I wasn't ready. At times, I told myself I would probably fail anyway. I had become skilled at talking myself out of opportunities before I ever gave myself a chance.

This wasn't random. It was a pattern rooted in years of feeling unseen, unworthy, and uncertain. The fear of being visible, the pressure, the risk, the weight of responsibility, made hiding feel safer. And so I stayed small. I watched others rise, including people with less experience and, sometimes, less ability. I comforted myself with the lie that I was "better off this way."

But the truth was, I wasn't better off. I was suffocating under the weight of all the potential I kept burying. The fear of failure had wrapped itself so tightly around me that I began to confuse playing small with being safe. I had to ask myself hard questions: Why do I feel the need to hide? Why do I doubt my voice? What am I really afraid of?

Answering those questions meant facing some painful truths. I had equated failure with shame. I had made rejection personal. I believed that staying silent and unseen would protect me from being exposed or judged. However, that mindset was shaped by old wounds and early experiences that taught me to keep quiet, to stay small, to stay safe.

Despite all of this, I built a meaningful career. Throughout my thirty-year career as a registered nurse, I have received several recognitions that attest to my dedication and the impact of my work. But even with these achievements, I hesitated every time leadership called.

One of my former managers saw something in me I couldn't yet see in myself. She encouraged me to pursue a management role, genuinely believing I had what it took to be a leader. But I couldn't receive it. I told myself I wasn't ready, that I didn't belong in that kind of position.

When I transitioned into education, the same pattern repeated. I was offered interview opportunities for leadership roles, as well as chances to shape the future of nursing through mentorship and vision. These were roles that aligned perfectly with my experience and qualifications. And yet, I still battled with self-doubt.

As I began doing the inner work, I slowly learned to speak life over myself. I started declaring my readiness, my value, and my right to take up space. That shift gave me the courage to finally apply for positions that reflected both my skill set and the doctorate I had earned.

Still, there were moments I fell back into the old pattern. I'd hear that familiar voice whispering, You're not qualified. And I'd have to remind myself: Yes, you are. You always were.

Breaking the cycle meant confronting fear head-on. I had to stop shrinking in rooms where I was called to stand in. I had to stop apologizing for my presence, my power, my voice. For too long, I waited for someone else to permit me to affirm what I already knew deep down: I was capable. I was prepared. I belonged. Not because I had it all figured out, but because God had been preparing me all along.

Leadership, I came to learn, has nothing to do with titles or perfection. Authentic leadership is rooted in character, by showing up with integrity, consistency, and a willingness to grow. It's about listening before speaking, taking responsibility when it's easier to deflect, and standing firm even when your confidence wavers. A true leader isn't someone who knows everything, but someone who leads with humility, honesty, and a genuine heart. It's the mother who rises early to pray over her children. The teacher who speaks life into a struggling student. The woman who, despite her fear, chooses to stand in truth and walk in purpose.

Authentic leadership is found in the quiet decisions no one sees and the brave steps no one applauds. It's trusting yourself enough to show up, shaky voice and all, because something greater is calling you forward.

Eventually, I made a decision: No more hiding. No more shrinking. No more letting fear or doubt narrate my story. I chose to rise, to take up space, to use my voice with purpose and power. I chose to believe in the worth God placed inside me, and to walk in it fully.

That decision changed everything.

Reflection Questions:

- What fears or beliefs have caused you to shrink back from opportunities meant to grow or elevate you?
- How have they shaped the way you see your value in professional spaces?

Journal Prompt:

Think of a moment when you hid your voice, downplayed your skills, or said "no" to something you were fully capable of doing. Write honestly about what held you back. Now, write a letter to that version of yourself, offering compassion, truth, and a new declaration: No more hiding.

Chapter Nine

AWAKENING STRENGTH: THE CATALYST FOR CHANGE

S tepping into leadership wasn't just about titles or positions; it was about reclaiming the parts of me I had silenced. Every brave "yes" became a seed of growth, proof that fear no longer ruled me. But something deeper was stirring. As I began to say yes on the outside, God was doing something powerful on the inside, awakening a strength I didn't know I had. What came next wasn't just about career; it was about transformation.

For much of my life, I carried the weight of old wounds and unspoken pain, not realizing how much they shaped how I showed up in the world. But healing has a way of cracking through the hardest ground. One day, a familiar verse began to echo differently in my heart: "Therefore, if anyone is in Christ, he is a new creation; old things have passed away; behold, all things have become new," (2 Corinthians 5:17).

I had heard it before, but this time, I believed it.

This wasn't just a spiritual truth; it was an invitation. A call to step into the life God always intended for me, not defined by trauma or shame, but shaped by grace, identity, and renewed purpose. I began to see that becoming new wasn't about erasing the past; it was about letting God rewrite what I believed about myself through His truth.

One of the most eye-opening moments in my healing journey came during a raw conversation with my daughter. We were talking about her childhood, and at first, her memories were warm, full of laughter, fun, and the kind of closeness I always hoped she'd remember. She told me I was a great mother. But then her tone shifted, and what she shared next felt as if it pierced my heart.

My daughter opened up about moments when I wasn't emotionally present, times she needed me, and I didn't show up the way she hoped I would. Her words were honest and brave. I could hear the pain behind them, and I knew she wasn't trying to blame me; she was trying to be seen and heard. That realization hit me hard.

One memory that was shared jolted me to my core, and everything inside me went still." She was nine years old and had worked up the courage to tell me something that no child should ever have to carry alone—that her father was having an affair. She told me how scared she was, how much her body trembled as she approached me. And then she reminded me of my response: "Okay," I said. And then I told her to go play.

Hearing that broke me. Seeing it now through her eyes was unbearable—it hurt deeply. She needed comfort, reassurance, and a sense of safety. Instead, I dismissed her. I didn't see it then. But I see it now.

As I sat with her words, I was transported back to my own childhood. I remembered the time when I opened up to my mother, when I exposed the truth about the shadow's predatory actions, only to be met with emotional distance. I had learned early not to expect emotional support. And without realizing it, I had passed that pattern on.

It devastated me to recognize the cycle. Not just because it hurt her, but because I knew that hurt. I had carried that same ache for years. And despite my love for my daughter, I had repeated what had been done to me. That truth was hard to face. I mourned it deeply.

For days, I carried a heavy sadness. I grieved the missed moments. I regretted the times I let my emotional wounds dictate how I showed up, or didn't, for the people I loved most.

But that conversation also became a turning point. It forced me to stop pretending that love alone was enough. Presence matters. Words matter, healing matters. And healing starts with honesty, with ourselves and with those we've hurt, even if it was unintentional.

Recognizing the pain I had caused wasn't the end. It was the beginning of change, real change. And that change started when I stopped hiding behind what happened to me and started taking responsibility for how I chose to move forward.

After that moment of clarity, something shifted. I began a deeply personal journey to understand who I was and what I was truly here for. It was as if a light finally penetrated the fog, and I realized I had reached my breaking point; something had to change. Enough was enough. I was no longer willing to live in a state of survival. It wasn't just about functioning anymore; I was ready to let go of old patterns and embrace a new way of thinking.

I realized I had reached my limit. Enough was enough. I was ready to let go of old patterns and embrace a new way of thinking. I need not only to function in this world, but also to flourish.

Now, in this chapter of my fifties, I find myself face-to-face with emotions I've carried for far too long, feelings of inadequacy, guilt, and self-doubt that had quietly taken up space in my heart. It became clear that if I wanted to grow, I had to break free from the weight of my past. I needed to name what was holding me back, so I could begin releasing its power over me.

I wish I could go back and change how I showed up in certain moments with my daughter. But I can't rewrite what happened. What I can do is choose how I live with those memories—how I let them shape me today. I can choose what meaning they hold in my life today. Because that's where healing begins, not in denying the past, but in redefining how it continues to shape my life now.

Those old shadows used to follow me into the present, showing up in how I saw myself and how I moved through the world. But I no longer let them dictate my direction. Instead of allowing trauma to set the course, I've started telling a new story—one grounded in truth, in growth, and grace.

For so long, I carried the weight of shame, insecurity, and silence, believing the lie that my voice didn't matter and my story held no value. I moved through life armored with self-protection, strong on the outside but breaking silently within. I thought strength meant pushing through, holding it together, never letting anyone see the cracks. But even in those dark and hidden places, God was there. He walked with me through it all, quietly, faithfully, never rushing, never leaving. He was patient with my pain, present in my confusion, and constant even when I couldn't feel Him. All the while, He was waiting for me to believe what He had already spoken over my life: You are chosen. You are loved. You are whole.

What I didn't understand then is that real strength isn't about striving; it's found in surrender. Surrender doesn't mean giving up; it means giving in to the one who already carried what I was never meant to hold. The shift came when I stopped trying to fix myself and started trusting the God who had been holding the pieces all along. The patterns I had lived under—fear, self-doubt, silence—began to break, not because I willed them to, but because I finally allowed God to do what only He could.

When he spoke, it wasn't through thunder or spectacle, it was through truth that felt like a gentle breaking open. It was steady. Compassionate. Firm, but full of love. The kind of truth that pierces, not to wound, but to free.

Now, I'm no longer living in reaction to what happened. I'm living with intention. I've chosen healing. I've chosen hope. And with every step forward, I'm learning that strength and surrender were never at odds; they were always meant to meet. Because it's in that sacred place, where I release control and receive grace, that God rewrites the story.

I believe now that the most powerful chapters of my life are still unfolding. And this time, I'm not just surviving them, I'm standing in them.

Reflection Questions:

- What moments in your life have revealed a deeper strength within you, one you didn't know you had?
- How has God used those moments to show you who you truly are beyond the pain or limitations of your past?

Journal Prompt:

Write about a time when you felt something shift inside you, when you started to see yourself differently, perhaps more clearly, through the lens of faith or growth. What truths are you beginning to believe about yourself now that you once doubted? What does "becoming new" look like for you today? Invite God into that space through your words. Let Him show you what healing, strength, and surrender can look like together.

Chapter Ten

THE LIGHT THAT CHANGED ME

The journey toward awakening doesn't happen all at once. It unfolds in layers; each act of courage, each quiet decision to believe in more, becomes a step toward light. And sometimes, that light finds us in the most unexpected moments, right in the midst of fatigue, fear, and the fragile hope that our lives could still become something beautiful. That's where I found myself, on the edge of something new, not yet sure if I had the strength to rise again, but refusing to give up.

Growing up, I never saw myself as exceptional. I wasn't the overachiever or the standout. I did what I was supposed to, turned in my work, and followed the rules. Deep down inside, I felt like I was trying to survive, to stay invisible enough not to cause any trouble, yet present enough to be considered good. One of my older siblings was often praised as the family genius, which he was, and in comparison, I quietly faded into the background. Not much was expected of me, and over time, I accepted the lie that I didn't have much to offer.

It took me nearly a decade to finish my associate's degree. Life kept interrupting, with financial strain, emotional turmoil, and the constant pull of survival. My brothers and I didn't have parents we could lean on. For us, education wasn't a guarantee; it was a privilege, a stretch, a fight.

By the time I was married to my children's father and pregnant with our second child, I had only one year left in my nursing program. I was overwhelmed, juggling motherhood, school, and the weight of what felt like an impossible dream. I was caught between the quiet joy of new life and the rising fear that everything I'd worked so hard for was slipping through my fingers. I was tired. I was scared, afraid that if I didn't finish, I wouldn't be able to support my family. I was caught between the joy of a new life and the fear that I was about to lose the future I had fought so hard for.

We made the heartbreaking decision not to continue the pregnancy. I still remember the day we went to the clinic. The chaos of the New York City subway, the shouting of protesters outside the building, the shame and confusion I carried like armor. And then, something happened.

A voice, calm and undeniable, spoke to my spirit: "Get up. I will work things out for your unborn child." I knew it was the Holy Spirit.

I turned to my ex-husband and said, "Let's go." He followed without a word. That moment changed everything. God honored that decision. My son was born during spring break, which was in March that year, the only window of time when I could be absent from school without penalty. I missed just one day. He wasn't due until April, but God made sure the timing worked out. It was a miracle.

From that day on, I trusted God on a deeper level. I couldn't unhear His voice. I couldn't deny His hand on my life. That whisper became an anchor, the reminder that I was seen, chosen, and covered. Even in my doubt, He had a plan. And that truth became the foundation of my strength.

It marked the beginning of everything that came next.

Reflection Questions:

- Have you ever experienced a moment when God whispered to your spirit, reminding you that you were seen, chosen, and covered, even in the middle of fear or uncertainty?
- How did that moment shift your perspective about yourself, your worth, or your future?

Journal Prompt

Take a moment to revisit a time when you felt like you were getting by, when survival felt like your only option. What lies did you begin to believe about your worth or potential in that season? Now, reflect on a moment when God's truth broke through those lies. What did He speak to your heart? How can you hold onto that truth today as a foundation of your strength?

PART THREE

Chapter Eleven

WALKING IN WHOLENESS

This part of my story marks another actual turning point, the moment I stopped running from the pain of my past and started walking toward the wholeness God always intended for me. It didn't happen overnight. Healing rarely does. But something inside me shifted. I began to recognize the lies I had carried for far too long and the patterns that kept me playing small.

For the first time, I believed, not just in theory, but deep in my spirit, that I was not only worthy of love and purpose, but already equipped by God to walk in them.

This is where I began to trust God's voice more than my fear. To stand, even when my knees trembled. To show up as myself, fully and honestly. And so, I started rewriting my story, not as the girl who faded into the background, but as the woman who chose to rise, to lead, and to live with intention.

What lies ahead may not be perfect, but it's mine. And it's real.

Wholeness, I've learned, is not the absence of brokenness; it's the courage to live fully, even with the scars.

Reflection Questions:

- Have you ever experienced a moment when God's light broke through your doubt, fear, or sense of control?
- What changed in you when you finally surrendered and chose to trust Him more deeply?

Chapter Twelve

GRACE THAT FOUND ME IN THE DARK

Even though the shadows of my past lingered for years, one truth remained constant: God never let go of me. Time after time, He showed up in quiet but undeniable ways. He sent people into my life who saw what I couldn't see in myself, my value, my strength, my potential. Through them, He reminded me that I wasn't alone. With each encounter, He gently pulled me out of the darkness, helping me rediscover joy and slowly rebuild my hope, one piece at a time.

I Couldn't Do This Alone

One of the most impactful people I met during a difficult season of my life was Rev. Joy Clarke, whom I encountered while living in Queens, New York. At that time, my children were still young, and I was walking through one of the hardest chapters I had ever faced. I was attending a small neighborhood church with my kids, not realizing how much I needed that space or how much healing would begin there.

The pastor, a wise and compassionate woman, became a powerful example for me. She didn't sugarcoat the truth, but she led with strength and grace. Her leadership gave me the clarity and direction I desperately needed.

For years, I lived in a home where tension was constant and peace felt out of reach. What began with moments of laughter and shared dreams eventually gave way to anger, control, and fear. Our home, once filled with light, grew dark and heavy with silence. I endured words that tore at my confidence and moments that left both emotional and physical scars.

I'll never forget one night, as I was preparing to submit my final paper for my Bachelor of Science in Nursing degree. After months of balancing motherhood, school, and work, I was determined to finish. But in an act of cruelty, the home computer I needed for my assignment was destroyed. I remember sitting on the floor, tears streaming down my face, praying for help. And God answered through a friend who sent her brother to repair the computer. Miraculously, my paper was recovered. I drove across the town that night and submitted it just in time. I graduated, not by chance, but by grace.

Even after that, the pain didn't stop. Words meant to wound still echo in my memory, but something inside me began to shift. I realized that staying in that environment was not protecting my children; it was teaching them to tolerate brokenness. I wanted them to know peace—to see what love rooted in safety looked like.

The church and that pastor became my refuge. Through her counsel, I began the slow, sacred work of healing. One piece of wisdom she shared stayed with me: "Never speak poorly about your children's father. They will understand in time." Her words grounded me. I learned that protecting my children meant guarding their hearts, even when mine was still mending.

With courage and prayer, I decided to begin again. I sold our home in Queens, packed our lives into boxes, and moved to New Jersey for a fresh start. It wasn't easy, but it was necessary. God met me every step of the way, confirming that this journey toward peace and wholeness was His will.

Even as we began anew, I made sure my children had the chance to maintain their relationship with their father. I wanted them to grow up free from bitterness, knowing that forgiveness is a gift we give ourselves. That choice became one of my most significant acts of strength—not just surviving the pain, but transforming it into purpose.

Even after all we had been through, I continued to make sure my children stayed connected to their father. I placed them on the Greyhound bus every other weekend and on school breaks, making it work however we could. And when my children were old enough to decide for themselves, I gave them the freedom to shape their relationship with him. That, to me, was love—protecting them without poisoning them.

It was in this season of rebuilding that I began to understand the strength found in vulnerability and the courage it takes to ask for help. I was no longer the girl who hid behind a smile, pretending everything was okay. I was a woman determined to heal, no longer afraid to admit that I couldn't do it alone. And once again, God showed up through people. He sent another pastor into my life—Rev. Provey Powell, Jr.—whose steady, truth-filled teachings became a constant, compassionate voice that spoke truth over me, reminded me of who I was in Him, and gently helped me believe in who I could become.

As my heart opened, so did my faith. I found deep comfort in Scripture, especially in the promise: "I will go before you and make the crooked places straight; I will break in pieces the gates of bronze and cut the bars of iron," (Isaiah 45:2). That verse became my anchor. It spoke to the very place I was in, lost in what felt like a maze of brokenness and fear. But here was God, declaring that He was already ahead of me, leveling the uneven ground, breaking through every barrier that stood in the way of my healing. It wasn't just about direction; it was about divine intervention. It was about a God who clears paths we can't even see yet and who lovingly removes the obstacles we never thought could be moved. That understanding changed everything for me.

Reflection Questions:

- Have you ever reached a point where you realized you couldn't keep going on your own?
- Who has God placed in your life to help carry the weight, and are you allowing yourself to receive that support?

Chapter Thirteen

THE STRENGTH OF SURRENDER

Learning to ask for help has been one of the most transformative steps in my healing journey. Those distractions, old habits, fear, shame, and even people who once held power over me, no longer define my direction. It taught me that vulnerability is not weakness, it's strength. Along the way, I realized how critical it is to stay focused, to protect my peace, and to stop allowing the shadows of my past to pull me away from the light of purpose, hope, and healing.

True Rest

One scripture that speaks deeply to my spirit is Hebrews 4:10: "For he who has entered His rest has himself also ceased from his works as God did from His." This passage reminds me that true rest, the kind that brings peace to your soul, comes not from striving, but from trusting in the finished work of Christ. It's not about giving up; it's about letting go of self-reliance and embracing the truth that I don't have to carry everything on my own. That kind of surrender marks the beginning of real healing.

Rest, I've come to learn, is not passive; it's deeply active. True rest takes faith. It means stopping the endless striving, releasing fear, anxiety, and self-doubt, and choosing instead to receive the peace that comes from knowing our worth is already secure in God's love. In this true rest, I've found real strength. Not because life got easier, but because I stopped trying to earn a value I already had.

God reminded me, and still reminds me, that I am enough. Not when I accomplish more. Not when I have it all together. Right now. Just as I am, but living in that truth required something deeper: clearing out the noise—the shame, the inner critic, the toxic stories I'd held onto for too long. That work was hard, but necessary.

Learning to rest in God's finished work meant protecting my mind and heart. I had to become intentional about what I allowed to shape my thoughts and spirit. This shift didn't happen overnight, but over time, true rest in God's promises transformed everything.

Writing this book has become one of the bravest things I've ever done. It cracked open a new way of living, one that allowed healing to take root and faith to grow. And through it all, I've learned to keep my eyes on the light ahead, refusing to let the shadows of my past steal my future.

Reflection Question:

What does "true rest" look like for you, beyond just physical rest, and what steps might you need to take to begin embracing that rest in your mind, heart, and spirit?

Chapter Fourteen

STEPPING INTO THE LIGHT GOD ALWAYS SAW IN ME

hadows marked my childhood, threats that felt constant, invisible, and unnerving. I didn't learn how to navigate danger or chaos; I just learned how to survive it. Over time, I became skilled at keeping the pain hidden, tucking away the fear, unmet needs, and silent wounds that would later demand attention in adulthood. I couldn't name it then, but I was living with a fractured sense of self, shaped by the belief that being unseen was the safest place to be.

Choosing To Rise

Adulthood didn't bring the relief I had hoped for. It became another battlefield, one where self-doubt screamed louder than truth. I internalized the lies that I was broken, unworthy of love, respect, or even kindness. I played roles that made others comfortable, often at the expense of my dignity. I learned to keep my head down, to serve, to endure, because somewhere along the line, I believed that's all I was meant for.

As life presented opportunities, moments to lead, to step forward, to be seen, I often pulled back. I told myself I wasn't ready or that someone else was more qualified. Promotions passed me by. Leadership roles went to others, and while I knew I had the skills, I couldn't silence the voice that kept whispering, You're not enough. I became my roadblock, sabotaging my potential out of fear that I would fail, or worse, be exposed as a fraud.

The truth was, I had what it took. I had the experience. I had the vision. But I didn't yet have the belief in myself. And so I kept playing small, shrinking from possibility, hiding my voice even when I had something powerful to say. Every time I whispered the question, "Am I enough?" I buried the answer; I was too afraid to believe.

For years, I wore shame like armor, believing invisibility was safer than vulnerability. I kept running from the woman I was meant to become, afraid she wouldn't be accepted or understood. But that fear didn't protect me; it paralyzed me, keeping me locked in cycles that only deepened my regret.

Now, I'm beginning to understand what it means to stand tall. It's not about never falling. It's about rising again and again. It's about finally choosing truth over fear. For the first time in my life, I'm choosing to rise. Not because I feel ready, but because I've realized the cost of staying small is far too high. Choosing to rise means deciding, again and again, that fear will not hold the final say over who I am or what I'm capable of becoming.

Reflection Question:

What does "rising" look like for you right now, and what is one small step you can take today to move toward that?

Remember, rising doesn't mean you have to be perfect or have all the answers. It simply means showing up for yourself, even when it's hard, and choosing to believe that your voice, your story, and your dreams matter. Each small step forward is a victory, and with every rise, you grow stronger, braver, and closer to the person you're meant to be. Keep choosing to rise.

PART FOUR

Becoming

There comes a moment in the healing journey when you stop just unpacking the past and start stepping into the future God intended for you. I'm not just understanding what happened—I'm owning who I am because of it. I refuse to live defined by brokenness. My pain, my resilience, my faith, they've all come together to make me whole. I see myself as God sees me, chosen, called, equipped, and deeply loved. This is where everything changes. This part of the journey is about owning that identity, recognizing the anointing that's been with me all along, and learning to live from that truth. This is where I rise and live from the truth that's been in me all along.

Chapter Fifteen
Identity & Anointing

I spent years defining myself by what I lacked, what I didn't have, who I didn't become, and the wounds I carried. But God never saw me through that lens. He saw me through the lens of purpose, identity, and anointing. This part of my journey is about shedding the false labels and embracing who I already am in Him: chosen, worthy, and called.

There have been times when I've cried out, "God, where are You in all of this?" When life felt unbearable, when betrayal and trauma clouded my vision, I longed for immediate rescue. I wondered why God didn't step in sooner, why He allowed certain storms to last so long. But as I've grown, I've come to understand something deeper: God moves according to His perfect timing, not our urgency. And in that timing, there is purpose.

Habakkuk 2:3 reminds us that, "For the vision is yet for an appointed time; But at the end it will speak, and it will not lie. Though it tarries, wait for it; Because it will surely come, it will not tarry." That promise has grounded me. It taught me that waiting isn't passive, it's spiritual preparation. It's trusting that even when nothing makes sense, God is still working behind the scenes.

Personal growth hasn't come easily. It's felt more like climbing a mountain than coasting through a breakthrough. Some days, the weight of my past threatened to pull me back down. But I reached a point where I had to make a decision: I could either carry what broke me, or I could trust God to rebuild me. And in that choice, I began to lay down the burdens I had carried from the shadow and the shadow I wore as armor. The trauma, the silence, the shame, and embrace the truth that I am more than what I've been through.

This chapter of my life is no longer about just surviving. It's about walking in the identity God gave me and recognizing the anointing He's placed on my life. I am not what happened to me. I am who He says I am, called, chosen, and equipped.

Do You Want to Be Made Well?

Healing isn't just about time; it's about choice. In John 5:6, Jesus asked the man at the pool, "Do you want to be made well?" It's a question I had to face myself. True healing required more than just understanding my pain; it required my participation. It meant surrendering what I was holding onto—fear, control, and shame—and choosing wholeness, even when it felt unfamiliar.

There comes a point in every healing journey when we are faced with a profoundly personal and confronting question: "Do you want to be made well?" This was the question Jesus asked a man who had been paralyzed for thirty-eight years, lying by the pool of Bethesda, (John 5:6). Imagine enduring nearly four decades of waiting, hoping for change, and perhaps even resigning to despair. Yet when Jesus approached, He didn't ask about his condition; He asked about his desire. Then he gave a command that still echoes across time: "Get up and walk" (v.8).

That invitation wasn't just for the man at the pool; it's for all of us. At some point, we each have to decide: Will we continue to live trapped by our pain, or will we rise above it? Will we stay stuck in cycles of regret, shame, and fear, or step forward into the wholeness God is offering? I came to that crossroads myself. And when I did, I knew I couldn't wait for someone else to rescue me. I had to partner with God in reclaiming my identity and future.

This was the beginning of a deep internal journey, one that taught me that healing isn't about becoming someone new but about returning to who God created me to be. Wholeness isn't a lofty ideal; it's a necessary reality. Our identity in Christ is not shaped by our trauma or the opinions of others. It is rooted in truth: that we are made in

God's image, woven together with intention and purpose. Each scar, each setback, each triumph—it's all part of a divine tapestry. Psalm 139:14 affirms it: "I will praise You, for I am fearfully and wonderfully made." I began to see myself through that lens, not defined by shame, but seen, known, and loved by God.

That shift led me to understand the power of anointing. In Scripture, anointing wasn't just a ritual; it was a sacred act that marked a person for a purpose. Kings, prophets, and priests were anointed with oil, a symbolic act that set them apart for divine use (see Psalm 20:6 and 28:8). Today, that same setting apart happens through the indwelling of the Holy Spirit. Romans 8:11 states, "But if the Spirit of Him who raised Jesus from the dead dwells in you, He...will also give life to your mortal bodies."

This anointing is not abstract. It's real. It's the power to rise when everything in your life tells you to stay down. It's divine protection, spiritual authority, and sacred affirmation. It is what breaks the yoke, the heavy burdens, the toxic cycles, the lies that keep us bound.

I've learned that the oil of God often flows from pressure. Just as oil is pressed from olives, there is beauty and power that can emerge from the crushing seasons of life. When I thought I was breaking, God was pouring something new into me. His anointing gave me the strength to confront my fears, the courage to walk in truth, and the vision to see myself not as broken, but as chosen.

I no longer wear shame as armor. I wear the anointing of God as a covering. And because of that, I can rise every day, not just to survive, but to lead, to love, and to live on purpose.

Chapter Sixteen

MOVING FORWARD

There comes a point when looking back is no longer the assignment. Healing prepared me, but now it's time to move forward, not perfectly, not without fear, but with faith. I'm learning to walk with boldness, to trust God's voice over my doubts, and to step into the future with clarity, grace, and a new kind of strength.

After relocating to the vibrant state of New Jersey, I embraced the journey of life as a divorced woman, raising my children amidst the challenges and joys that accompanied our new chapter. Years slipped by unnoticed, and before I realized it, a decade passed in the blink of an eye. It was during this time that I serendipitously met a remarkable man who would soon become my husband, a relationship that has flourished over the past fifteen years.

Throughout my life, my heart has often been filled with a yearning for companionship, but God's embrace has been ever-present, as if refusing to let me slip away into loneliness. My exploration of faith deepened, fueled by reading the

Bible, participating in enlightening Bible study sessions, and drawing inspiration from powerful messages delivered by another extraordinary pastor whom God put me in a position to meet.

I encountered this dynamic pastor after meeting my current husband. One of our first dates was unforgettable; he took me to his home church in Maryland, a journey that required commitment since it was not just around the corner from my New Jersey home. Every Sunday, this devoted man would drive to pick me up, showcasing his dedication as we worshipped together.

At the beginning of our relationship, I was cautious about introducing him to my children. I wanted to ensure that our connection had genuine potential and that his intentions were true. So, I planned our meetings for weekends when my children were away with their father or engaged in extracurricular activities. To my relief, he never complained and was always willing to meet me wherever I suggested. His reliability and consistency were a breath of fresh air.

Less than a year into our courtship, he surprised me with a heartfelt proposal. What I cherished most about him—though he was not perfect, no one is—he was perfect for me. He boldly professed his love for God, and time and again, he proved himself to be a dependable partner.

When he finally met my children, he seamlessly stepped into the role of a supportive figure, never shying away from the responsibilities that came with being a part of our blended family. Instead of feeling overwhelmed, he helped lighten the load of parenthood, offering assistance and companionship as I navigated the complexities of being a working, divorced mother.

In him, God provided a protector and provider, someone who made our burdens a little lighter, helping me to shoulder the weight with grace and understanding. Above all else, I felt an overwhelming sense of safety whenever I was with him. His presence hugged me like a warm blanket, offering both comfort and reassurance—the steady warmth of someone who truly valued me.

Reflection Question:

As you reflect on your journey, where do you sense God inviting you to stop surviving and start becoming, stepping into your true identity, healing, and purpose?

PART FIVE

Chapter Seventeen

SHE IS NO LONGER SILENT

I spent years working through the layers of silence, survival, and shame, but now, something has shifted. I'm not just healing anymore. I'm stepping forward. Reclaiming. Emerging.

Earning my Doctorate in Educational Leadership was one of the proudest moments of my life. It came through perseverance, late nights, sacrifice, and deep conviction. I was the first in my immediate family to do it. And still, there were moments when the old feelings crept in, feelings that told me I didn't belong, that I needed to shrink to be accepted, and that I shouldn't expect to be seen.

I remember sitting beside another woman, both of us having earned the same title. Yet only one of us was addressed as "Doctor." That moment said more than words ever could. It was a quiet erasure of effort, of identity, of worth. But this time, I didn't internalize it as truth. I recognized it for what it was: a reflection of how the world sometimes fails to honor women who look like me, walk like me, and rise like me.

Still, I rise.

I'm no longer looking for permission to exist in full view. I no longer wait for validation to claim the space I've earned. I know who I am. I am educated, yes. But I am also equipped. I am called. I am powerful. And now I'm learning to speak from that place, not with arrogance, but with clarity, conviction, and humility.

This is not just about titles. This is about voice—about refusing to hide my strength or soften my presence to make others comfortable. The silence that once shielded me has now been shattered by truth. I am walking with purpose. I am living out my anointing. And I am no longer silent.

I've started setting firm boundaries and walking in greater transparency, places where I once allowed others to shape how I saw myself. I'm finding the courage to speak the truth; to let go of the shame I never should have carried in the first place. I was not the predator. I was not the one who caused the harm. I was the one who endured and survived.

I no longer measure my worth by the shadows of my past. Slowly, steadily, I'm stepping out—not to be seen by others, but to finally see myself. To accept all of me: the scars, the wisdom, the strength. Every step I take now is a step into wholeness.

I'm emerging. Not just recovering, but becoming. The shame and self-doubt that once clung to me are losing their grip. I'm learning to embrace the woman God created me to be, strong, capable, and worthy. I am no longer shrinking. I am standing in the light, not just to exist, but to rise.

I now recognize how self-sabotage quietly interfered with my growth. Walking away from opportunities and criticizing myself too harshly was fear disguised as protection. But naming these patterns has become my turning point. I am choosing growth. I am choosing resilience. This journey isn't just about what I've overcome; it's about what I'm building.

This is the strength of a woman: fierce, rooted, and rising. I will no longer apologize for who I am. The shadows that once swallowed my voice will not define the rest of my story. Enough is enough. It's time to shine beyond the shadows. I'm not hiding anymore. I'm not shrinking. I'm stepping into the light with clarity, boldness, and hope. The past may have shaped me, but it no longer controls me. I am reclaiming my voice, my power, and the future God has prepared for me.

Chapter Eighteen

THE HIDDEN SANCTUARY

Throughout my faith journey, I have embraced a multitude of lessons, each one etched into my heart. Some were gently whispered during quiet moments of prayer, while others resonated boldly through the transformative voices of those God had placed along my path. One voice that continues to resonate profoundly is that of my current pastor, Rev. Provey Powell, Jr, whom I first encountered through my husband. He was the one who officiated our marriage, imparting wisdom and grace through many of his teachings. His teachings have flowed into my spirit like a river, rich and life-giving, long before he even realized the full weight of the truths he was sharing. Each message has nurtured my soul, guided my steps, and deepened my understanding of faith.

One of his teachings that left a lasting imprint on my soul came from Psalm 91, the Psalm of Protection. He spoke of a hidden sanctuary, a sacred place beneath the shadow of the Almighty. It was more than poetic language; it was a truth that pierced through years of fear and hiding. For so long, shadows had felt like places of danger and silence for me. But Psalm 91 invited me to see shadows from a different perspective. Under God's shadow, I wasn't unseen. I was covered.

Pastor may not have known the connection his words were making in my heart, but God did. That's what happens when God speaks; His Word goes forth and never returns void. I realized then that not all shadows are meant to be feared. Some are holy. Some are healing.

What once felt like a place of concealment became, for me, a place of refuge. The same shadows that once symbolized pain and silence were now transformed into a reminder of God's divine protection. I began to understand that He had never abandoned me in the dark; He had been sheltering me, shielding me, preparing me. I wasn't just surviving in the shadows. I was being kept.

This was more than a revelation. It was a restoration. I discovered that the hidden place described in Psalm 91 is not only a shield, but also a space of belonging. A refuge where I am wrapped in God's love, guarded by His faithfulness, and strengthened by His promises. It's where fear begins to fade and courage takes root. Where healing flows, not because the world gets easier, but because His presence grows deeper.

In that secret place, I encountered God as protector, healer, and Father. I came to know that His angels surround me, His grace sustains me, and His truth sets me free. And if that were all, it would be more than enough, but He gives even more. That sacred space is also where I found salvation, strength, and peace that the world cannot give or take away.

That is something worth celebrating. That is where I rise from.

Thoughts:

In the shelter of God's shadow, I found more than protection; I found perspective. What once felt like hiding became holy ground. And now, as I step out with greater clarity and courage, I carry with me the lessons shaped in that sacred space. What the Lord taught me was not just for surviving, but for learning how to live life fully.

Chapter Nineteen

LESSON LEARNED: LIGHT AFTER THE FALL

This journey has taught me more than how to heal; it has taught me how to live. Each chapter of my story held its lesson, and every scar became a seed of wisdom. What once threatened to silence me has now become the foundation of my voice. In the pages that follow, I share the truths that reshaped my life, lessons on success, freedom, wholeness, self-love, and what it truly means to walk in victory.

I used to believe that my past disqualified me from making a meaningful impact, that I was too broken, too scarred, and too far gone. That belief kept me bound in silence and shame. But I have since learned a powerful truth: God doesn't discard our pain. He repurposes it.

Every fall, every failure, every heartbreak has held a hidden lesson, waiting to be uncovered, healed, and shared. What once felt like disqualification has become my calling. The very places I once wanted to forget have become platforms for ministry, empathy, and connection. Our struggles are not the end of the story; they are the soil where purpose begins to grow.

God has a way of taking the very thing that tried to destroy us and using it to strengthen others. He pulls us out of the pit, not just for our healing, but so we can reach back and walk with others through theirs. What we once saw as weakness becomes a witness. And what once made us feel small becomes the very thing God uses to shine through us.

Where I used to isolate, I now lean in as endless opportunities. Where I used to shrink, I now stand. Not because I have it all figured out, but because I understand now that light shines brightest through those who've come through the dark.

In Matthew 5:14, the Bible says, "A city that is set on a hill cannot be hidden." I no longer hide who I am or where I've been. I've been lit by grace, and I choose to let that light shine in every space I enter, for everyone who still believes they're too broken to rise. I am living proof that God can use it all.

This is what it means to emerge, not perfect, but fully present. Not untouched, but transformed. The woman I was always meant to be is no longer buried under shame. She is rising, radiating hope like morning light, with a story worth telling and a purpose worth living.

Chapter Twenty

LIGHT AFTER THE SHADOW

How do you reclaim your voice after years of silence? You begin by listening, not to the wounds of the past, but to the quiet truth that has been buried inside you all along. You don't ignore the fear or the doubt, but you stop letting them speak louder than hope. Even if your voice shakes, you speak because each word becomes a declaration that silence no longer holds the final say.

And what do you do with the shadows that have haunted you? You stop running from them. You turn and face them with the light of truth. You realize they only existed because your light was always present, hidden, but never extinguished. You were never meant to stay small, silent, or unseen. You were meant to shine.

So here I am, reclaiming my voice, not as a reflection of past pain, but as a witness to present strength. No longer invisible, I'm stepping fully into the light, releasing shame and embracing the life God intended for me. My story isn't one of defeat; it's one of rising. I am not the sum of what I've endured. I am the product of God's redemption, growth, and a resilient womanhood that refuses to be silenced.

I've let go of the lie that I was too damaged to be useful. I now understand that God doesn't waste pain; He recycles it into purpose. My journey is proof that healing is possible, that transformation is real, and that light can—and will—shine after the shadow. Until God says my story is done, I will continue to rise, trusting that every scar can become a signpost of His grace.

Redefining Success

The moment of transformation didn't come with fanfare; it came like dawn after a long night. Quiet, steady, undeniable. I woke up to the truth that the version of success I'd been chasing wasn't mine; it had been shaped by fear, silence, and survival.

Looking closely, I began to see how self-sabotage had woven itself into my decisions, how my past had quietly told me to play small, stay safe, remain unseen. That awareness became the first crack in the fog. It didn't erase the pain, but it gave me a way forward.

Spiritual awakening often feels like emerging from a deep sleep. At first everything is blurry, and then suddenly, you begin to see how much grace has been surrounding you all along. That's what it felt like. God had been with me in every hidden place, blessing me in ways I hadn't recognized. When my eyes finally opened, I saw the life He'd been waiting for me to claim.

From that place of clarity, I made a decision: I would stop being a spectator in my own life. I would no longer let fear take center stage. Love, not fear, would lead. And I would carry that light not just for myself, but for others still stuck in the dark.

Each step forward became sacred. Not because I had everything figured out, but because I was choosing to live, not just survive. I began to see myself differently: not broken, but blooming. Not inadequate, but equipped. My journey became more than recovery; it became a testimony.

I now know that success isn't measured by titles or applause. It's found in alignment with purpose, in the quiet courage to heal, to hope, to believe again. Success, for me, is walking in truth, no longer hiding, no longer shrinking, but living fully in the light of who I am and who God says I've always been.

Stepping into the light didn't erase every battle, but it changed how I saw myself and my journey. I began to see through God's eyes. That's when the breakthrough came, breaking the grip of what had held me back for years. I had to find the courage to step out from behind the shadows. And you will, too. Your shadows may be fear, shame, regret, or anything else that dims your light and keeps you from fully living. They limit your potential and block the promises God has for you. But when you take that step of faith and push past them, you open yourself to His truth and His promises, like this one: "Arise, shine, for your light has come, and the glory of the Lord rises upon you." (Isaiah 60:1, NIV)

The more I stood in God's truth, the clearer it became; this was never just about surviving my past. It was about rising above it, redefining faith, and claiming victory in every area of life, love, and purpose. I refused to keep chasing someone else's definition of success. Instead, I began to live fully from the unshakable truth God had already planted in me, a truth that was destined to break through and bloom.

There was a time when I measured success by how much I could achieve, how perfectly I could perform, or how well I could keep everything together. But that version of success always left me empty, striving, exhausted, and unseen. It wasn't until I allowed God to reshape my definition of success that I began to truly live. Success, I've come to learn, isn't about proving my worth; it's about walking in the worth that was already given to me. It's not about climbing ladders, but about standing firm in grace. It's the quiet courage to heal, the strength to forgive, and the freedom to show up fully, flawed, loved, and whole.

God's grace was the turning point, the breath that stirred life into places I thought were long gone. His love didn't just restore me; it revealed me. My worth was never lost, only buried under years of silence, shame, and survival. What I once believed disqualified me has now become the very evidence of His power. My identity isn't shaped by my scars but by the strength that rose from them.

When I finally declared, "Enough is enough," something broke loose in me. I stopped apologizing for taking up space. I stopped shrinking to fit places that couldn't hold the fullness of who I was becoming. That moment wasn't about perfection; it was about liberation. I no longer measured myself against the shadows of my past. Instead, I let the contrast reveal my light. And in that light, I began to shine, not despite the darkness I came through, but because of it.

Letting go of comparison has been one of the most freeing decisions of my life. My journey may not look like anyone else's, but it's mine, marked by resilience, healing, and the undeniable fingerprints of grace. These scars? They're not signs of defeat. They're proof that I've endured, I've grown, and I've overcome. I no longer wait for someone else to validate my success; I celebrate the woman I'm becoming. Every hard lesson, every *no* that led to a better *yes*, every time I chose truth over silence—all of it is part of the masterpiece God is creating in me.

I rise today, not because everything is perfect, but because I've been awakened. I've stopped living like a woman still bound by her wounds. I've started living like a woman redeemed, reclaimed, and revived. My voice is no longer a whisper; it's a declaration. I am walking in the light, no longer running from who I was, but stepping boldly into who I was always meant to be.

Success, for me, has been completely rewritten. It's no longer about titles, applause, or status. It's about the quiet confidence that comes from being in step with God. It's about spiritual maturity, inner peace, and living every day rooted in purpose. His voice has become my compass, guiding me not to impress others, but to honor Him with my life.

That clarity didn't come overnight. It took surrender. It took learning how to hear God's voice amid both storms and silence. I didn't pursue Him out of obligation; I chased after Him because I needed to know I was loved. And He met me there, again and again, with a love so steady and healing it taught me how to love myself.

First John 4:19 says, "We love Him because He first loved us." His love taught me how to extend grace to my own heart, how to stop rehearsing old shame, and how to live in the fullness of who He created me to be.

Redefining success has also meant learning the power of forgiveness, especially toward myself. Jesus didn't just die for part of my story; He covered it all. He forgave me fully, and through His example, I learned that holding on to guilt and regret was never meant to be my burden to bear. Forgiveness is freedom, and freedom is success.

So no, I didn't get here on my own. Every breakthrough, every moment of clarity, every step forward has been nothing but God. His strength lifted me when mine ran out. His grace caught me when I stumbled. His love kept calling me forward when I wanted to hide. These victories aren't just mine; they are living proof of His faithfulness.

Today, success means waking up knowing I am deeply loved, already enough, and chosen by God. It means living honestly, walking boldly, and staying close to the One who called me out of the shadows. That's my success story, written by His hand, filled with His breath, and reflecting His glory.

Declaration:

I declare that I am no longer bound by old definitions of success that were rooted in shame, comparison, or silence.
I am divinely equipped, deeply loved, and fully seen by God.
My story is not one of brokenness, but of beauty rising from the ashes.
I walk boldly in the light of God's truth,
Rooted in grace, guided by purpose,
And confident in the woman I was always meant to be.
This is my time to rise, to shine, and to thrive.

Chapter Twenty-One

LET FREEDOM REIGN: A NEW BEGINNING

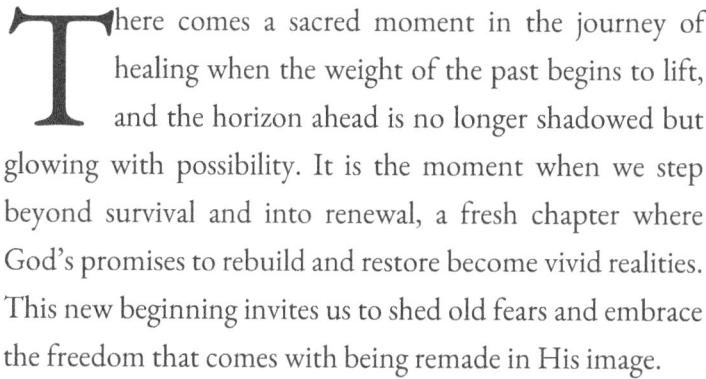

There comes a sacred moment in the journey of healing when the weight of the past begins to lift, and the horizon ahead is no longer shadowed but glowing with possibility. It is the moment when we step beyond survival and into renewal, a fresh chapter where God's promises to rebuild and restore become vivid realities. This new beginning invites us to shed old fears and embrace the freedom that comes with being remade in His image.

In this space between what was and what is yet to be, we find the courage to open our hands and hearts, ready to receive the abundant life God longs to give. It is here that freedom begins—not as a distant hope but as a present power, breathing new life into every corner of our soul.

With this renewed spirit, we begin to walk boldly into the light of God's unwavering love, letting go of what once held us captive and embracing the fullness of who we are called to become.

The profound wisdom expressed in the Bible resonates deeply within my spirit, particularly the verses found in Jeremiah 31:3-4, which declare, "Therefore with lovingkindness I have drawn you. Again I will build you, and you shall be rebuilt." This passage beautifully illustrates the promise of renewal and restoration. The journey to allow God to rebuild us hinges on two essential truths.

Firstly, we must wholeheartedly embrace the depth of God's unconditional, unearned, and unwavering love. This divine affection remains steadfast through every season of life, providing a solid foundation that nurtures our souls amid uncertainty and turmoil.

Secondly, I have come to realize the transformative power of serving and giving to others. Shifting our focus outward not only alleviates the weight of our struggles but also fosters a profound sense of connection and purpose. Engaging in acts of kindness and service holds the remarkable potential to uplift those around us while simultaneously elevating our self-esteem in ways we might not initially anticipate.

Additionally, I have come to understand that expressing one's truth, particularly when it demands tremendous courage and unflinching honesty—offers a powerful opportunity to embrace one's authentic self. This courageous act of vocal honesty can be profoundly liberating, granting you the freedom to articulate your experiences and emotions without the weight of fear holding you back. By cultivating a heightened awareness of the delicate areas in our lives where we might falter, we place ourselves in a position of strength and resilience, fortifying ourselves against the adversarial forces that threaten our inner peace.

I now realize that if I truly desire to experience God's profound influence in my life, I must take proactive steps and make intentional strides forward. God's love should not merely exist as a transient thought; it must resonate deeply within the core of our being, igniting a transformative fire within our souls. In return, this divine love illuminates our life's journey, guiding us with a sense of purpose and clarity that guides us through even the darkest of times.

When I look in a mirror, I now see myself. I don't see a broken woman; I don't see a woman ruined by someone else's predatory action. I don't see unworthiness. I no longer emit the familiar fumes of vulnerability, but instead an undeniable sweet fragrance fills the air.

The road to victory may have begun in brokenness, winding through moments of confusion and loss. Yet, through God's transforming light, that same road has become clear and full of purpose. Once I wandered in the shadows, unsure of my direction; now I walk with confidence, knowing that I have been carried by grace.

"For we are to God the fragrance of Christ among those who are being saved and among those who are perishing," — 2 Corinthians 2:15.

I carry that fragrance of life. I am not lost.

I am His—redeemed, restored, and victorious.

The road to victory may have started crooked, but through God's transformative guiding light, it is now wide open. I was once lost. I have moved beyond the shadows, "I am found." My heart is filled with promise when I read 2 Corinthians 2:16 which says, "To the one we are the aroma of death leading to death and to the other the aroma of life leading to life. And who is sufficient for these things?" I am!

Your restoration is coming.

Our journey with Christ can yield a vibrant harvest that shatters the chains keeping us captive for years, bringing blessings not just to us but also to our children and grandchildren for generations to come. My path has been a profound expedition of breaking free from those invisible shackles, stepping boldly out of the shadows, and embracing the radiant light that dwells within me. Now, I feel a deep calling to share that illuminating light with others who may be struggling.

It's your time to shine, your moment to rise in the fullness of your victory. Join me in this sacred, rhythmic dance of freedom. Let your feet move to the heartbeat of the drums, each beat echoing strength, liberation, and joy. Feel the rush of excitement as it swells within you; let the warmth of this moment wrap around you like sunlight breaking through the clouds. The breeze plays on your skin, twirling through your hair like a whispered promise of renewal.

I envision a community that nurtures the soul—a place where those once silenced reclaim their voices with boldness and grace. A space where resilience is not just spoken, but lived, where those who have felt broken, forgotten, or unsure of their worth find sanctuary and strength. Here, we rise together. We heal together. We remember who we are and reclaim the power we were always meant to carry. In this sacred space, we don't just survive, we soar. This is our journey, one of healing, hope, and radiant empowerment.

I want others to see that they, too, can rise. They, too, can rewrite their narratives. They, too, can embrace the wholeness of who they are, free from the weight of past mistakes or unhealed wounds.

This is more than just my story; it is an invitation. This is an invitation to you. An invitation to step forward, to find strength in your vulnerability, and to embrace the hope of a new beginning. We are defined by how we rise, by how we reclaim our voice, and how we shine, unapologetically and without restraint.

This is our journey. This is our light. And together, it's our time to shine.

This is the call. This is the moment. This is your invitation.

Together, we shine. And **this**, this radiant, rising, joy-filled journey, is only the beginning.

Chapter Twenty-Two

EQUIPPED FOR THE JOURNEY: WALKING IN REAL SUCCESS AND LASTING VICTORY

Real success isn't about applause or achievement by the world's standards. It's about becoming who God created you to be. It's living with purpose, rooted in your identity in Christ, and moving forward, no matter how broken the past may have been. Victory is already yours through Christ, but walking in it takes intention, healing, and truth.

Here's how to equip yourself for the road ahead, one honest step at a time:

1. Renew Your Mind with the Truth

Most battles start in the mind. The enemy uses doubt, fear, and shame to make us feel unworthy and stuck. However, God's truth gives us the power to break that cycle.

His Word reminds you of who you are, even when your feelings or past try to say otherwise.

Try this:

- Start your day by reading a short Bible passage about your identity in Christ (Romans 8, Ephesians 1 are great places to begin).

- Write down three biblical truths or affirmations and say them out loud daily. Example:
"I am chosen." (Ephesians 1:4)
"I am not condemned." (Romans 8:1)
"I am more than a conqueror." (Romans 8:37)

- When a negative thought pops up, stop and replace it with scripture.
Instead of: *"I'll never get it right,"* say: *"I can do all things through Christ who strengthens me." (Philippians 4:13)*

2. Step Out of Hiding and into Your Calling

Shame, fear, and comparison can keep us quiet. They make us believe that our story doesn't matter or that someone else is more qualified. But God gave *you* a voice for a reason. You have something to offer, even if you're still healing.

Try this:

- Share a small piece of your story with someone you trust. Healing often starts when we stop hiding.

- Get involved in something that brings you joy and helps others, whether that's mentoring, serving at church, or just showing up consistently.

- Say "yes" to that thing you've been avoiding because it feels too big. Sometimes the discomfort is just growth in disguise.

3. Find a Safe, Supportive, and Faith-Filled Community

You weren't made to go through this alone. Healing and growth occur most effectively in a safe and honest community. People who remind you of who you are in Christ, pray with you, and speak life into you are a gift. Ask God to help you find them.

Try this:

- Join a small group, Bible study, or online faith community where people are real, not perfect.

- Ask someone you trust to be a prayer partner or mentor. Let them walk with you.

- When things feel heavy, don't isolate. A simple message like, *"I'm struggling today, can you pray for me?"* may be the first step toward a breakthrough.

4. Live from the Victory Jesus Already Won

You don't have to earn God's love or strive for worthiness. Jesus already paid the price. The cross covers every failure, and His resurrection gives you the power to live free today. Instead of living in shame or regret, you can choose to live in grace and truth. The victory has already been won; you have to walk in it.

Try this:

- Write a letter to yourself from God's perspective, one that speaks His love, mercy, and forgiveness over your life. Read it when shame tries to creep back in.

- When guilt or regret resurfaces, take communion privately as an act of remembrance. Let it remind you of Christ's finished work and your freedom in Him.

- Keep a *Victory Journal*. Record the moments God answered prayer, opened a door, brought peace, or reminded you that you are His.

5. Commit to Walking in Confidence Every Day

Confidence isn't loud or showy. It's quiet, trust that God is with you, working through you. Some days that confidence looks like bold steps; other days it's just showing up when you don't feel strong. Either way, choosing to walk forward, especially when it's hard, is powerful.

Try this:

- Begin each day with this prayer: "God, help me walk confidently in who you created me to be."

- Dress with intention, even if no one sees you. Showing up for yourself helps shift your mindset.

- Set one bold goal every week. Whether it's applying for a job, sharing your story, or starting a new habit, take one step that stretches your faith.

Final Encouragement

Becoming equipped for success and victory isn't about perfection. It's a daily decision to believe what God says about you and to act like it's true, even when it feels hard. Each day you choose to be intentional, speak the truth, live on purpose, stay connected, and walk in grace, you're building a life that reflects God's power at work within you.

You already have what it takes, because God is with you. Now it's time to live like it.

It's Time to Shine Beyond the Shadows

You are not the sum of your past. You are not defined by your worst days, your insecurities, or the things you wish you could undo.

- You are called.
- You are equipped.
- You are ready.

I know what it's like to feel stuck. I know what it's like to wonder if anything will ever change. But I also know what it's like to get back up, to speak life over your broken places, and to walk with a quiet strength that can only come from God.

If he did it for me, He can do it for you.

So rise.

Shine.

Take your next step.

The victory is already yours; let's live like it.

I've come to believe this with my whole heart: it doesn't matter how or when you begin, what matters is that you do start. What matters is what you choose to do with what God has placed in you. The victory has already been secured. Your role is to rise and walk in it. So whatever shadow you've been living under, whether it's shame, fear, silence, or self-doubt, know this: it no longer has power over you. The moment you decide to move forward, you're stepping into victory. And you don't have to do it alone. Let's stand together. Let's walk in the freedom God promised. Let's dance in the victory that's already ours.

Chapter Twenty-Three

THE LIGHT WITHIN: FREE AND WHOLE

The Final Chapter

Strength and hope were never out of reach; they were always there, even in the silence, even in the struggle. They are within reach for you, too.

This is not just my story; it's a testimony to what happens when we stop running from the pain and start trusting God with the pieces. When Jesus said, "It is finished," He meant it. The shame, the fear, the lies we believed about ourselves—none of it has the final word. What once looked like a mess has been transformed into a miracle, not just for me, but for others who will see my healing and begin to believe that theirs is possible, too.

Justice Belongs to the Lord

For a long time, I waited for justice. I carried a wound that wasn't mine to bear, left by someone who tried repeatedly to take what they had no right to take. That shadow from my past followed me into adulthood, whispering that I was broken, dirty, or somehow to blame.

I lived under that weight for years. I wondered if there would ever be a reckoning, if the pain would ever be seen for what it truly was. I held onto fear, confusion, shame, and unanswered questions, aching for closure. But then I learned something that changed everything:

Justice isn't mine to carry. It belongs to God.

"Dear friends, never take revenge. Leave that to the righteous anger of God. For the Scriptures say, 'I will take revenge; I will pay them back,' says the Lord," (Romans 12:19).

The person who harmed me now lives in confusion and torment, caught in a reality I didn't orchestrate, but that doesn't bring me peace. Peace came when I let go. I don't need revenge to be free.

True justice is freedom.

Freedom came when I released my grip on the one who hurt me.

Freedom came when I gave my pain to the One who heals.

I no longer carry shame that was never mine. I no longer let fear or trauma define my worth. I have been restored, not through someone else's punishment, but through God's grace and truth. That is justice. That is victory.

A Journey to Wholeness

Absolute freedom came when I stopped punishing myself for what happened. I finally understood that what was done to me didn't change my value. Beneath the pain, I was still whole; I just had to believe it.

Freedom meant quieting the inner critic that told me I wasn't enough. It meant listening instead to the voice of truth, the one that said I was worthy, strong, and made with purpose.

I learned that freedom does not just escape, it's *arrival*. It's breathing without heaviness. It's loving without fear. It's hoping again. It's standing in your truth, with your head held high, knowing you no longer have to hide.

"Freedom is the oxygen of the soul." – Moshe Dayan

And I breathe it deeply now.

I've found joy, not in perfection, but in the process of becoming. I've found peace, not in the absence of struggle, but in accepting who I am today. I've found hope, not in knowing the future, but in trusting the One who holds it.

Freedom is no longer just a distant dream; it's my daily reality. It's how I speak to myself. It's how I love others. It's the light within me that no longer flickers, but shines steady and strong.

I've stepped out of the shadows. And I will never go back.

This is freedom.
This is wholeness.
This is me.

The book of Joel reminds us of a powerful truth: God restores.
"I will restore to you the years that the swarming locust has eaten," (Joel 2:25).

We all have "locusts" in our lives—seasons, people, or choices—that devoured our peace, stole our time, or tried to destroy our identity. But God never intended for us to remain broken or barren. He meets us right where we are, in the ashes, and calls us to rise. Through resilience, faith, and surrender, restoration becomes more than a possibility. It becomes a promise fulfilled.

God's faithfulness isn't confined to biblical times. It showed up in my life when I least expected it, when I thought all had been lost. He healed the places I had long written off as too broken to mend. And in His timing, He brought someone into my life who embodied His love in ways I never thought I would experience.

My husband became the tangible reflection of God's grace, a man of steady strength, unwavering commitment, and quiet courage. He didn't turn away from my wounds; he honored them. He didn't just love the parts of me that were whole; he stood guard over the parts that were still healing. His love didn't rescue me; God had already done that, but it reaffirmed the truth I had begun to believe that I was worthy, cherished, and safe.

He showed up, not just in the good times, but in the hard moments. When I doubted my voice, my purpose, or God's plan for me, he reminded me of who I was becoming. His faith in me mirrored the way God loves, steady, sacrificial, and without condition.

Chapter Twenty-Four

A LIFE REDEEMED, A FUTURE SECURED

When I look back on my life, I see more than pain; I see the hand of a Redeemer who never let go. The girl who once questioned her worth, who wrestled with her identity, who struggled for nearly a decade to earn a simple associate's degree, now holds a Doctorate. That's not just education, it's restoration.

God didn't just restore what I lost; He multiplied it. He brought beauty from ashes, poured grace over shame, and gave me a future I never dreamed I could claim.

Even my 96-year-old Auntie, Shelah Liverpool, wise and honest, once said to me, after hearing of my doctorate: *"I never expected that from you."*

And she wasn't wrong.

Not because I lacked potential, but because I had hidden my light for so long. I believed the lies. I stayed small. And how could anyone else see what I couldn't yet see in myself?

But God always saw me. And he sees you, too.

He doesn't just repair what's broken, He rebuilds with purpose. Wrapped in His righteousness, I walk forward not in pride, but in peace, knowing that my life is proof of what happens when we stop letting the past define us and start walking in His promises.

A New Wineskin: Transformed for God's Purpose

In Mark 2:22, Jesus said, "And no one puts new wine into old wineskins...but new wine must be put into new wineskins."

This verse isn't just about change, it's about transformation. God doesn't pour fresh purpose into a heart that's still bound by bitterness, shame, or fear. He invites us to let go of what no longer serves us so we can become vessels fit for what's next.

God didn't just patch up my life; He made me new.
He calls me beloved.
He calls me chosen.
He calls me whole.

The past no longer defines me, mine or anyone else's. Christ lives in me. And when shadows try to creep in, His light leads me out. I've exchanged the old wineskin—the limiting beliefs, the self-hate, the generational pain—for a new one, made to carry joy, purpose, strength, peace, and unshakable love.

And now, I extend this invitation to you:

Let go of the old. Make room for the new.

What God has prepared for you is fresh, pure, and filled with His purpose. You don't need to carry what He already freed you from. Lay it down. Open your heart. Let Him transform you into something powerful and renewed. Light and life are inextricably interwoven. You cannot have life without light. From the very beginning, God revealed this truth to us. When the world was dark, empty, and full of chaos, His first words were, "Let there be light" (Genesis 1:3, NIV). Light was His starting point. It was the foundation for everything else. The moment light appeared, order began to replace chaos. Creation responded. The seas are filled with life. The earth released what had been hidden in the soil, and seeds began to sprout and flourish.

That same principle applies to us. Without light, God's light, our lives remain in the shadows, full of confusion and unanswered questions. But when His light breaks through, everything changes. What once felt barren begins to grow. What seemed dead comes alive. Hidden potential begins to rise because His presence reveals what He planted in us all along. Just as in the beginning, light brings life. And that life is yours when you step into His light.

Will You Make Room?

I want you to know that things happen when God speaks, and things happen when people speak what God has already spoken. Even more amazing, things happen in those who receive what God says, namely, the word of God. As we journey toward wholeness, take one small step, and God will take the next. I pray this book has been more than just words. I pray it has stirred something within you, a quiet awakening, a reminder that your story is not over, that your healing is possible, and that your light deserves to shine.

Your journey doesn't have to look like mine. But I believe there will come a moment, maybe today, maybe tomorrow, when you'll stand up and say, "Enough is enough." And when that moment comes, know this:

You are not alone.
Your pain doesn't disqualify you.
Your healing is ahead of you, not behind you.
And God has already made a way.

As Isaiah 60:1 (NIV) declares:
"Arise, shine, for your light has come, and the glory of the Lord is risen upon you."

So rise.
Shine.
Take your next step.

And let the legacy of your life be one of redemption, resilience, and radiant hope.

What's Coming Next

I'm so honored you've walked this far with me, and the journey isn't over yet. I invite you to stay close and keep your heart open for what's ahead. The companion workbook, *It's Time to Shine,* is now available, created to help you apply what you've read and walk more fully in your healing, growth, and transformation. It's filled with powerful prompts, reflections, and space to process all that God is unfolding in your life.

Stay tuned. There's more goodness and grace ahead.

I would be honored to walk alongside you and your community on this journey of healing, hope, and renewal. I am available for speaking engagements and consultations on a variety of platforms, including churches, women's conferences, retreats, podcasts, book clubs, and summits. Whether you're gathering a group or seeking personal support, I also offer both group and individual sessions designed to create space for reflection, transformation, and growth.

If you're interested in inviting me to speak or would like to schedule a session, please visit: www.authorgracelnorris.com.

Or reach out via email: sgnorris58@gmail.com

Let's take this next step together. Your breakthrough is waiting.

Scripture References

(Formatted according to the Chicago Manual of Style)

Unless otherwise indicated, Scripture quotations are taken from the Holy Bible, New International Version® (NIV). Copyright © 1973, 1978, 1984, 2011 by Biblica, Inc.™ Used by permission. All rights reserved worldwide.

Additional Scripture quotations are taken from the following versions:

- New King James Version (NKJV). Copyright © 1982 by Thomas Nelson. Used by permission. All rights reserved.

- New Living Translation (NLT). Copyright © 1996, 2004, 2015 by Tyndale House Foundation. Used by permission of Tyndale House Publishers, Inc., Carol Stream, Illinois 60188. All rights reserved.

- New Century Version (NCV). Copyright © 1987, 1988, 1991 by Thomas Nelson, Inc. Used by permission. All rights reserved.

All Scripture references have been carefully selected to encourage reflection, healing, and transformation in alignment with the mission of this workbook.

ABOUT THE AUTHOR

Dr. Grace Liverpool-Norris, EdD, MSN, RN, is a passionate faith-based speaker, author, mentor, educator, lay leader, health professional, and trauma survivor whose calling is to help others rise from the shadows of shame, self-doubt, and generational pain to live whole, bold, and empowered lives. Through her deeply personal storytelling and Spirit-led teaching, Dr. Grace inspires others to break cycles, embrace healing, and rediscover the power of their voice.

She is the author of *Beyond the Shadows: The Light Within* and creator of its companion workbook, *It's Time to Shine*, designed to guide others on a sacred journey of transformation through reflection, forgiveness, and faith. Dr. Grace's speaking platform is rooted in faith, honesty, hope, and the belief that even our most painful experiences can be transformed for a greater purpose.

Dr. Grace holds a doctorate in educational leadership and a master's degree in nursing. She brings wisdom, compassion, and clarity to every space she enters, equipping individuals and communities with the tools to rise beyond their past and live with renewed purpose.

Rooted in her faith and shaped by her personal and professional journey, Dr. Grace inspires others to shed shame, embrace their identity, and step boldly into the life God has prepared for them. Whether she is mentoring one-on-one, speaking on a stage, or facilitating healing spaces, her voice resounds with the truth that wholeness is possible, and it begins from within.

To connect with Dr, Grace visit:
www.authorgracelnorris.com. Or reach out via email:
sgnorris58@gmail.com

www.ingramcontent.com/pod-product-compliance
Lightning Source LLC
LaVergne TN
LVHW092321110226
831513LV00012B/433